Making Space

Raising hidden voices of the Swedish LGBTQIA+ community

Authors: Kabir and Rachel McDonald

Publisher: BoD – Books on Demand, Stockholm, Sweden

Printer: BoD – Books on Demand, Norderstedt, Germany

ISBN: 978-91-7699-724-6

Authors: Kabir and Rachel McDonald

Editor: Stina S. Lundin

Project leaders: Kabir and Rachel McDonald

Contributors: Zeynab Peyghambarzadeh (Writer), Eliott "Wyrneck" Karlsson (Illustration), Charlie Rytterlund (Illustration), Evelina Svärling (Translation), Moa Strinnö (Translation), Sanna Forsberg (Transcribing), and Sumaiya Hafsa (Transcribing)

ACKNOWLEDGEMENTS

The project team would like to thank all the people that made this project and book possible. Firstly, to the board of SFQ that supported this project idea from 2015, assisted in writing a project application in 2016 and then continued to help the team with organization, networking, and advertising of the project during 2017.

A special thank you goes to Daniel Dannfors and Linda Hörberg for managing the financial side of this project and to Stina S. Lundin for taking time to edit this book.

SFQ is extremely thankful to MUCF, Myndigheten för ungdoms- och civilsamhällesfrågor, the Swedish Agency for Youth and Civil Society, who granted the financial support needed to see this project through.

Thank you sincerely to the participants, collaborators, and to everybody that has come to the lectures, workshops, and meetings across Sweden during 2016 – 2017.

SFQ: Swedish Federation of LGBTQIA+ Students

In English

The Swedish Federation of LGBTQIA+ Students is a national federation for norm criticism and LGBTQ-perspectives in higher education. SFQ has local branches throughout Sweden's universities and colleges. The organization works to better the situation for people that are marginalized by hetero- and cis-norms. For example, lesbian, gay, bisexual, trans, intersex, asexual and queer students at Sweden's universities and colleges. Through educating on intersectional norm-criticism the organization advocates nationally and locally with a focus on cis- and heteronormativity in higher education. SFQ also educates and creates debate about the consequences that these norms have for students, studies, and the study environment.

As of summer 2017, there are eight active local branches spread all over Sweden. SFQ is a queer feminist organization believing in an intersectional approach to work against discriminatory structures. The SFQ work includes educating on LGBTQ issues at universities and university colleges, fighting heteronormativity within the academic sphere, in both the educational contents as well as in the study environment. SFQ's local branches are in Umeå, Stockholm (4), Örebro, Gothenburg, and Malmö.

For further information or to get involved with the federation: info@sfq.nu

SFQ: Sveriges Förenade HBTQIA+ -studenter

På svenska

Sveriges Förenade HBTQIA+-studenter (SFQ) är riksförbundet för normkritik och HBTQIA+-perspektiv i högskolan, med lokalavdelningar runt om på landets universitet och högskolor. Förbundet arbetar för att förbättra situationen för personer som marginaliseras av hetero- och cisnormer, exempelvis homo- och bisexuella, transpersoner, intersexuella, asexuella och queera personer som studerar vid Sveriges universitet och högskolor. Genom intersektionell normkritik bedriver förbundet påverkansarbete nationellt och lokalt med fokus på cis- och heteronormativitet i högre utbildning, samt utbildar och skapar debatt om dess konsekvenser för studenten, studier och studiemiljö.

Från och med sommaren 2017 finns det åtta aktiva lokala avdelningar spridda över hela landet. SFQ är en queer feministisk organisation som tror på ett intersektionellt sätt att arbeta mot diskriminerande strukturer. SFQ:s arbete omfattar utbildningar om HBTQIA+-frågor vid universitet och högskolor, att bekämpa heteronormativitet inom den akademiska miljön, både i utbildningsinnehållet och i studiemiljön. Våra lokala avdelningar finns i Umeå, Stockholm (4), Örebro, Göteborg och Malmö.

För mer information och kontakt med förbundet: info@sfq.nu.

TABLE OF CONTENTS

CHAPTER 1: BACKGROUND

The idea for this project grew from SFQ's need to see a LGBTQIA+[1] community that is representative of the movement's diversity. The project team wanted everybody to see themselves represented and wanted everybody to be seen and heard. The LGBTQIA+ community is diverse on many levels, and it is tiring to see only one homogenous group represented and heard at prides, meetings, and in the news. Therefore, this project came into place.

In the current years, SFQ has been actively working with the questions of inclusiveness and intersectionality. SFQ's previous project *Avslöja heteronormen! 2014 – 2015*,[2] (in English: Reveal the hetero-norm), and *Examensbevis i fokus, 2015*,[3]

---

[1] An umbrella term that is used to describe the community. LGBTQIA+ is the acronym used by SFQ since the start of 2017. LGBTQIA+ is an abbreviation for different identities: lesbian, gay, bisexual, trans, queer, intersex, and/or asexual. The plus (+) is used to illustrate that our community is more diverse than just these labels/identities as there are many more identities regarding sexual and romantic attraction and gender identity/expression than are included with the letters "LGBTQIA". Other common abbreviations used today are LGBT, LGBTI, and LGBTQ with or without the plus.

[2] Lundin, Stina, (ed.), Strömberg, Elise & Fuentes Araya, Catalina, Sveriges Förenade HBTQ-studenter, project report, *Avslöja heteronormen!: En undersökning om cis- och heteronormer vid universitets och högskolors verksamheter 2014-2015*, (Stockholm: SFQ, 2015).

[3] Sveriges Förenade HBTQ-studenter, handbook, *Examen i rätt personnummer: En handbok från Sveriges Förenade HBTQ-studenter om utfärdande av nytt examensbevis efter ändrad juridisk könstillhörighet*, (Stockholm: SFQ, 2015), 3.

(in English, Degree certificate in focus), derived from SFQ's understanding of the need for inclusiveness and intersectional analysis. The project Examensbevis i fokus investigated and compiled university and college's procedures, routines, and attitudes when issuing a new degree certificate after a graduate had changed their legal gender (and therefore personal number) in Sweden. In the project Avslöja heteronormen! SFQ used intersectional analysis to show how cis-heteronormativity is reinforced in higher education, as well as that many equality plans or policies made LGBTQIA+ identities and experiences of racism and racialization invisible by not describing these experiences even though it affects a large group of students.[4] There were stories about non-white students stereotyping white-Swedish norms against "other" (non-Swedish) norms on sexuality,[5] in other words, assuming that it would be less accepting to have a non-normative sexuality / sexual orientation when you are non-white. Even one story about how a person had specifically excluded a university based on their white-normative marketing (lack of representation of different skin colors) and another student that explained how they constantly needed to go into defense-mode as they were the only racialized student in their class.[6] Furthermore, there were other stories that highlighted white-normativity at university, for example, the use of racist course material.[7]

Through the project *Making Space*, SFQ wanted to expand SFQ's work further by critiquing the normative representation of the Swedish LGBTQIA+ community and by raising voices from the student community to represent this diversity. When SFQ received the grant from MUCF and started the ball rolling, the project team brainstormed a significant name for the project that will summarize the

---

[4] Lundin, Strömberg & Fuentes Araya, *Avslöja heteronormen!*, 121-122.

[5] Fuentes Araya, Catalina, "Intersektionalitet", in *Avslöja heteronormen!*, Lundin, Strömberg & Fuentes Araya, 37-38.

[6] Lundin, Strömberg & Fuentes Araya, *Avslöja heteronormen!*, 39; 134-135.

[7] Lundin, Strömberg & Fuentes Araya, *Avslöja heteronormen!*, 132.

needs and aims of this project. Thus, the name *Making Space: Raising hidden voices of the Swedish LGBTQIA+ community* came into play.

The acronym LGBTQ+ was used in the project name when the project started instead of LGBTQIA+ as when the team began the work in 2016 SFQ was known as Swedish Federation of LGBTQ Students and the team wanted the project name to reflect SFQ's name. To acknowledge the diversity within the community and be more inclusive of the identities from the diversity in the community the project team used the "+" sign. However, during the duration of this project, SFQ acknowledged the importance of being inclusive to marginalized parts of the community, people that identify as intersex and/or asexual are often made invisible, therefore I and A were added to make these two groups more visible. SFQ also wants to include other identities in the acronym that further represent the diversity in the community, the best way that SFQ could do this now was to add the "+" sign to symbolize other identities within the community.[8] Therefore, throughout this book, the acronym LGBTQIA+ has been used when referring to both to the project work, research and the community at large.

This project Making Space is done in English so that it can be available to the non-Swedish speaking people as well. As an organization SFQ has many international students, and students that have recently moved to Sweden, who do not speak Swedish which will also be benefited from this project. The project believes that having materials in English will complement those materials that already exist in Swedish and other languages, as a way of building the knowledge base for those who do not know Swedish. It also empowered the project team to get involved in this project, as they couldn't have done this together if the project language was in Swedish.

---

[8] "Notice: SFQ's name change and inclusiveness," SFQ, Last modified May 23, 2017, http://hbtqstudenterna.se/namechange2017/.

Therefore, SFQ hopes that this project has and will help empower others that do not currently see themselves represented to get involved in the LGBTQIA+ movement. By this the project hopes that LGBTQIA+ people living in Sweden will be motivated to join a local organization as a member, e.g. our own organization SFQ or another LGBTQIA+ organization or to become an activist here in Sweden. SFQ acknowledge that fighting for inclusivity is complex work, and that is why SFQ hopes that people who are currently active continue to fight for more inclusive spaces for LGBTQIA+ people. This project is for you, to know that you are not alone, and that together we are strong. SFQ sees a future LGBTQIA+ community that is diverse and representative. SFQ wants everybody to feel welcome and motivated to join the LGBTQIA+ movement regardless of how your body looks or what it is capable of, regardless of what you believe in or which religious views you have, regardless of whether you speak Swedish, regardless of how your family relations are, and regardless of your sexual or gender identity (or lack thereof) and regardless of where you are from.

Another part of this project was to build a network for Swedish LGBTQIA+ organizations. The aim of this network was for organizations to plan their work on racism and together make the LGBTQIA+ movement accessible to more people. As this is an ongoing process, it is not addressed further in this book. The project team has held meetings with other organizations and has held lectures and workshops at pride festivals throughout July 2016 to September 2017. The lectures covered the background and aims of the project, the findings from the research, and the workshops covered how to create more inclusive and safer spaces for the diverse LGBTQIA+ community.

This project aimed to bring academic knowledge from feminist theories and LGBTQIA+ activism on the same platform. SFQ started the project by pointing out that even though the LGBTQIA+ community is heterogeneous, there is a homogenous representation of the LGBTQIA+ community in the media, prides and leaders. This project wanted to raise voices that have not previously been heard in the understanding of the situation of LGBTQIA+ people in Sweden. By lifting the perspective from students with a non-Swedish and/or non-white background this project wished to create a greater understanding of the discrimination that these LGBTQIA+ students encounter. Through that, this project wanted to come to a point where the Swedish LGBTQIA+ movement can work together, long term, to get a more representative participation of people from different socio-cultural and religious groups with a changed approach.

A central term of this project is space. Based on different feminist theories,[9] the project team defines space as the embodiment of our ideas, activities, and perception time and place. We all, who are LGBTQIA+, live in our own cultural-social-religious-political-economic-academic-activist spaces but again we all are part of the bigger common space, which is Sweden and LGBTQIA+ community. This project used the words space, community, platform and groups interchangeably. This project wanted to bring the experiences and stories of people from diverse cultural-social-religious space to one common space: the Swedish LGBTQIA+ community by making a safe space for the diversity of voices. This is where the significance of the project name stands. This project is about making safe spaces for the people who either get unnoticed or are subject to stereotyping by already existing norms and perceptions about their own communities.

Another central part of this project's work is to see the LGBTQIA+ community is represented with diverse identities. The word representation can mean different things depending upon the context it is used within. For the purposes of this book representation is used as a term to describe a deliberate process

---

[9] Eagleton, Mary, (ed.), *A Concise Companion to Feminist Theory,* (Oxford: Wiley, 2003); Butler, Judith, *Gender Trouble: Feminism and the Subversion of Identity,* (New York: Routledge, 2006), 79-149.

consisting of two parts. The first part of this process is giving people who face marginalization the space they need to talk about their experiences and to own these experiences. This is what this book aimed to create, for this purpose this book is the space. Further in the book there are many stories from voices that are otherwise hidden. The second part of this process is increasing the diversity that is represented in both the media and within LGBTQIA+ organizations, so that a more accurate image of the LGBTQIA+ community in Sweden is seen. This is a central part to this entire project. The project team have tried to increase the representation through sharing diverse stories on social media, raising the findings from the research in media, and contacting other LGBTQIA+ organizations to ask how they are working on issues of representation, racism, and discrimination.

Making Space does not only mean that SFQ wants all people to find their own space to express themselves in the Swedish LGBTQIA+ community, but also means that SFQ wants those who are already taking space, to acknowledge their privilege and to help the Swedish LGBTQIA+ movement create space for hidden voices. *Making Space* is a collaborative action, and SFQ hopes that by raising hidden voices the whole community can get onboard and make the Swedish LGBTQIA+ community safer and more welcoming for all LGBTQIA+ people in Sweden.

The existing lack of understanding and space for diverse identities, alongside the rise of the right-wing extremist movement in Sweden and anti-immigration political agenda in Sweden and Europe have motivated the project team to do this work. This because, these things affect the LGBTQIA+ community in Sweden. The project team and others from SFQ are aware of the need for it through what we have heard from others and experienced ourselves in our time within SFQ and the wider LGBTQIA+ movement in Sweden. This project is a product of all of that and much more. It is a product of a growing anti-racist movement, women's movement, the never-ending fight for refugee and immigrant rights, intersectionality and norm critique as activism, and LGBTQIA+ activism.

This book is a product of the qualitative research done as a part of this project. The research presented is based upon interviews with students that have a non-Swedish or non-white background.

Research Aim

The aim of this research is as followed: How homophobia, transphobia, biphobia, and similar forms of discrimination, and racism, are experienced and maintained within the social spaces that non-Swedish and/or non-white LGBTQIA+ people living in Sweden move within.

This research presents a deeper intersectional understanding of how different levels of struggles, discrimination and violence are faced by LGBTQIA+ people who are non-white and/or non-Swedish and living in Sweden. Instead of using homophobia, transphobia, biphobia and similar forms of discrimination this book uses *LGBTQIA+ phobia*. This book uses this term as a more inclusive term to describe the struggles, discrimination and violence faced by LGBTQIA+ people.

This research was important for the project team to address since SFQ wants to see a student community that is representative of the diverse LGBTQIA+ community. However, SFQ has seen that there is a lack of understanding within the LGBTQIA+ community when it comes to the experiences of those that are discriminated against both because of where they come from, or the color of their skin, on top of the LGBTQIA+ phobia that all LGBTQIA+ people experience. It is this discrepancy which the project aims to address and understand through this research.

CHAPTER 2: DISPOSITION

This book is divided into 8 chapters. Chapter 3: Definitions presents the terms that are helpful for understanding this book and it also presents the feminist theories that this research is based on. Chapter 4: Methodology presents and contextualizes the aim of the research and describes the research methods that were used. Chapter 5: The Qualitative Analysis presents the results based on the interviews that were the basis of the research. In this chapter, the analysis is intertwined with the results and are presented through the feminist theories frameworks. Chapter 6: Profound Examples compiles examples of quotes that illustrate an overall picture of the interviewees experiences which go over the boundaries of the sections within Chapter 5. Chapter 7: Bi Invisibility in Sweden and Academia: From the perspective of an Iranian Activist, is a separate chapter written by an Iranian activist. The project team saw the need to create space for an expert to write from their perspective, as the issue of bi-invisibility came up during the interviews but the project team did not have enough information to draw conclusions from this. Chapter 8: Closure summarizes the findings of chapter 5 to 7 and presents the conclusions of this research. This book ends with recommendations to the way forward through discussing the following questions: Internal norm-critique and self-reflection and How can we make more inclusive and safer spaces for the diverse LGBTQIA+ community in Sweden.

CHAPTER 3: DEFINITIONS

In Section 1, the terms that are relevant for project and help the reader to understand the book are presented. In section 2, the theories and concepts that are used in this research are presented.

SECTION 1: TERMS

Cisnormativity, cisgender

Cisnormativity reinforces the static gender binary (that there are only two genders: men and women) which is also the basis of heteronormativity.[10] This norm assumes that a person's gender identity and/or gender expression is the same as the gender that was assigned to them at birth.[11] Cisnormativity works to make people with trans, intersex, and genderqueer experiences/identities invisible. Cisgender and cis are terms used to describe a non-trans person.[12]

Culture

---

[10] Lundin, Strömberg & Fuentes Araya, *Avslöja heteronormen!*, 17.

[11] "Glossary," RFSL, last modified October 26, 2015, http://www.rfsl.se/en/LGBTQ-facts/LGBTQ/glossary/.

[12] "Glossary," TGEU, last modified July 4, 2016, http://tgeu.org/glossary/.

Culture can be viewed as the values, norms, and the meaning of existence that a group of people create through a way of living. Culture is learned or created by a group of people in a given space and time.[13] For example, taking fika breaks with friends or colleagues is an example of a cultural phenomenon common in Sweden.

Ethnicity

This definition is taken from the discrimination law in Sweden. The law defines ethnicity as an individual's national or ethnic origin, skin color or other similar characteristic.[14] National origin means that people have the same national affinity, such as Swede, Sami or Chilean. Ethnicity refers to how you identify or experience yourself. It is the individual themselves that defines their ethnicity (ethnicities) from their background and their own individual history.[15]

Gender identity and gender expression

This definition is not taken from the discrimination law in Sweden, because the Swedish law includes the word "överskridande" which roughly translates to "cross". This is excluded from SFQ's definition since the word implies that there is a boundary to cross over.[16] Moreover, the authority for anti-discrimination in Sweden, Diskrimineringsombudsmannen (DO), defines gender identity as a person's own understanding of their gender and gender expression as how a

---

[13] Kluckhohn, Clyde, Untereiner, Wayne & Kroeber, Alfred, Louis, *Culture: A Critical Review of Concepts and Definitions,* (Cambridge: The Museum, 1952), 53-54.

[14] 1 kap. 5§ diskrimineringslagen (2008:567).

[15] "Etnisk tillhörighet som diskrimineringsgrund," Diskrimineringsombudsmannen (DO), last modified May 15, 2017, http://www.do.se/om-diskriminering/skyddade-diskrimineringsgrunder/etnisk-tillhorighet-som-diskrimineringsgrund/.

[16] 1 kap. 5§ diskrimineringslagen (2008:567); Lundin, Strömberg & Fuentes Araya, *Avslöja heteronormen!,* 18.

person expresses themselves with e.g. clothes, make-up, hair, and body language.[17]

Genderqueer

This describes a person who identifies as being between or beyond the gender binary. In other words, a person that identifies as neither only man/male nor only woman/female.[18]

Heteronormativity

This norm shapes how society thinks about gender, sex, sexuality, families and relationships. Heteronormativity assumes that there are only two genders, cismen and ciswomen, and that these are opposites to each other. For example, the hetero-norm leads to the expectation from society that cismen are masculine and attracted only to ciswomen, whilst ciswomen are feminine and attracted only to cismen. Heterosexuality is reinforced by the hetero-norm, and is therefore seen as the "normal" sexuality.[19]

Queer

This is a term that has several meanings, but within this book it is used to refer to the critique of the hetero-norm and/or the gender norm. It is also used by activists

---

[17] "Protected grounds of discrimination," Diskrimineringsombudsmannen (DO), last modified June 16, 2017, http://www.do.se/other-languages/english-engelska/protected-grounds-of-discrimination/.

[18] RFSL, "Glossary."

[19] RFSL, "Glossary"; Lundin, Strömberg & Fuentes Araya, *Avslöja heteronormen!*, 17; "Glossary Beginning with H," ILGA-Europe, accessed August 29, 2017, https://www.ilga-europe.org/resources/glossary/letter_h.

and individuals as a label to describe their own or other's non-normative gender identity, gender expression, and/or sexuality.[20]

Pronoun

In many languages, including both English and Swedish, people use pronouns when talking about other people or things. In case of people, these pronouns can include (but are not limited to) he, she, they, or ze. This book used the pronoun 'they' where it was needed to uphold anonymity of the participants.

Racism, Racialized, Racialization

Racism is an oppressive power system where particular groups in society are disadvantaged because of their skin color, religion and/or ethnicity.[21] Racism is structural and dependent on a power-structure and norms about race and ethnicity, it is a way to discriminate. Racism is experienced by individuals and groups in society that are racialized. This process is known as racialization. Racialization can occur both in single acts of racism and as a social process and these processes of racism and racialization impact how we see each other and ourselves.[22]

Second-generation Swedish citizens

This book defines people who were born and brought up in Sweden to parents who were not born nor brought up in Sweden as second-generation Swedish

---

[20] RFSL, "Glossary"; Ambjörnsson, Fanny, *Vad är queer?*, Andra utgåvan, (Stockholm: Natur & Kultur, 2016).

[21] Fuentes Araya, in *Avslöja heteronormen!*, Lundin, Strömberg & Fuentes Araya, 27.

[22] Gans, Herbert, J., "Racialization and racialization research," *Ethnic And Racial Studies* 40 (September 2016), 341-352.

citizens. This is to make a distinction between those who moved to Sweden as adults, since this distinction is relevant for the project, especially in terms of language and visa/citizenship status. However, this project wants to make clear that there is just as much variation within these groups as between them in terms of other experiences. The project also recognizes that this term can be problematic when used to label certain groups of Swedish people as the "other", in direct comparison to normative "white Swedes", see more about this in chapter six, section one.

SECTION 2: THEORIES AND CONCEPTS

Space, Time and Entity

Space can be referred to both physical and social spaces. There are public and closed and/or private spaces. For example: streets can be example of public spaces, a classroom can be example of a closed space and a bedroom can be an example of closed and private space. Here, all these three examples are physical space which has its own social structures, so they can be viewed as both physical and social space. With the advancement of technology, we now also have digital spaces. Space and time are two very crucial components in understanding social constructions of identity from the perspective of feminist theories.[23] Based on where and when a body is located it gets perceived and judged by its surroundings. For example, an intersex body in South Asian context has a cultural understanding which was historically associated with the entertainment culture. But, if we think, about Sweden in present time, an intersex body might have their own different cultural, social, and political struggle. The term space is frequently used throughout this book, the project team viewed cultural-social-religious communities as cultural and social spaces. The project team also viewed social media as the representation of digital space. Moreover, in relation to space and time, the word entity is used to describe a body embodied in norms and entangled in performances in certain spaces.

Intersectionality

Intersectionality is a tool that is used within social science research and by activists to analyze and understand different power structures and how these intersect with norms in a given group.[24] Intersectionality is even a way of looking at how

---

[23] Eagleton, *A Concise Companion to Feminist Theory*.

[24] Lundin, Strömberg & Fuentes Araya, *Avslöja heteronormen!*, 26; Lavizzari, Anna, *Intersectional Research Report*, (IGLYO, 2015), 5.

different power structures are related with one another leading to a pattern of social inequality.[25]

We are all affected by different norms because society is built upon norms. We have discussed this earlier as well that, norms dictate who is seen as normal and who is seen as abnormal, and are influenced by who has power and who is powerless. Each of us are complex entities that have different layers of identity.[26] We can therefore be influenced by norms of gender and/or sexuality in one way and norms of ethnicity in another. Many of us are both bearers of norms and breakers of other norms at the same time, depending on which setting we are in, and who is judging us.[27] An individual is always at an intersection, between different norms. Hence the word intersectionality.

In this project, intersectionality is a concept contributing to a framework based on other feminist theories to work with intersectionality. Specifically, for this project, intersectionality is about layers of performances (performance is explained later in this chapter) and experiences that one has in contrast with the spaces the person moves within. For example: A cis-woman who is black, severely visually impaired, and homosexual, who lives in Sweden has her own experiences which are unique. These different experiences in the different spaces, and different layers of their identity, in Sweden may have different consequences and may therefore be perceived differently from her white male homosexual peer who has a normative body functionality.

It's not that we create labels such as 'black', 'white', bisexual', 'able', or 'woman', to further divide us, but sometimes these labels are needed to give words to show

---

[25] Yuval-Davis, Nira, "Intersectionality and Feminist Politics," *European Journal of Women's Studies* 13 (2006), 193-209, http://dx.doi.org/10.1177/1350506806065752.

[26] The Association for Women Rights in Development, "Intersectionality: A Tool for Gender and Economic Justice," *Women's Rights and Economic Change* 9 (August 2004), 1-8.

[27] Lundin, Strömberg & Fuentes Araya, *Avslöja heteronormen!*, 26.

how we are perceived and how we experience the world and how our reality reinforces these labels. It is very important to understand the different layers of performances and experiences, to have an intersectional perspective. Therefore, this book is using such labels within this text to help to illustrate the diversity and the power struggles that exist within the LGBTQIA+ community in Sweden.

This project primarily included specific layers that highlights the cultural, ethnic and religious diversity within LGBTQIA+ community in Sweden. Because, one of the main aims for this project is to give those that aren't represented space to tell their story. Therefore, we exclusively recruited participants that would represent people who experience racism, and/or who are not born in Sweden, and/or who are from an underrepresented religion, ethnicity or culture in Sweden.

Norms

Norms shape what is accepted by a given society or group as "normal" and therefore steer the accepted way to behave or think. Norms are created and maintained by stereotypes and prejudice, whilst at the same time rewarding normative identities with different types of privilege and social status. Norms are therefore related to power structures. Every individual interacting in a space is related to another individual in some sort of power structure.[28] Power structures give some groups of people privilege over others, most usually those that follow norms have more power than those who do not follow norms.[29] To give an example from the findings of the project's research: Speaking Swedish is a norm in Sweden, so this gives a Swedish speaking individual a higher social status and

---

[28] Foucault, Michel, *The History of Sexuality: Volume 1 an Introduction,* (New York: Vintage Books, 1990).

[29] Lundin, Strömberg & Fuentes Araya, *Avslöja heteronormen!,* 19.

the privilege of e.g. more job opportunities and therefore more power in society, compared to someone who does not speak Swedish and who has to juggle the struggle between find work and surviving in Sweden and study the Swedish language. Power structures also create norms, they are not only product of norms.[30] Often norms change over time and space. Norms are often taken for granted and therefore invisible, it is usually only when someone (or a group) doesn't follow a norm that it is seen.[31] For example, one effect of the hetero-norm is that people who identify as heterosexual are not expected to "come out" whereas people who identify as non-heterosexual are expected to "come out" from heterosexual to another sexuality.

Norm critique, norm criticism

A method of focusing on the structure of society's norms with the aim to reduce discrimination and inequality. Norm criticism is used to make norms visible by showing and describing how norms work, highlighting the benefits and sanctions of following or breaking norms, and critiquing their existence or influence over minority groups in society.[32]

Performance and performativity theory

Judith Butler has explained gender from her theories of performativity.[33] She showed us how our bodies perform under certain norms and create identities for

---

30 Foucault, The *History of Sexuality.*

31 Lundin, Strömberg & Fuentes Araya, *Avslöja heteronormen!*, 16.

32 Lundin, Strömberg & Fuentes Araya, *Avslöja heteronormen!*, 16; RFSL, "Glossary".

33 Butler, Judith, "Performative Acts and Gender Constitution: An Essay in Phenomenology and Feminist Theory", *Theatre journal* 40, (1988): 519-531; Butler, *Gender Trouble*, 79 - 149.

themselves and for the society.[34] Our bodies are not independent bodies out of the context of space, time and social construct. Butler argues that, under certain social contexts our bodies perform in certain ways, thus we create the idea of gender of bodies.[35] For example, in certain culture applying makeup is considered as femininity in public social context. In those social context, a body that applies makeup can be perceived as a feminine entity by the wider society. Therefore, the applying make-up gets labelled as a sign of femininity. Butler argues that a body's identity is created in a constant circle of performances and the body is perceived by the wider society based on the social construct, norms and contexts in a certain space. When a body performs in certain way the society then judges if it is carrying certain assigned signs and if it is passed as certain gender. For example, if a cis-man wears makeup in public spaces in Sweden, he may not always pass as a cis-man.

This research took that understanding of performances and performativity to understand the participants' experiences and how they act under those experiences and contexts. For example, the project team questioned how a non-white homosexual body is performing in a stereotypically white and heteronormative social structure. Here, the context and wider space is Sweden, time is the present time, and smaller spaces are the cultural-social-religious spaces the body belongs to or are associated with. Based on that, this research identified norms that surround the participants in their regular life.

Master suppression techniques (MST)

The five Master Suppression Techniques are a norm critical tool that was first

---

[34] Butler, "Performative Acts and Gender Constitution", 519-531; Butler, *Gender Trouble*, 79 - 149.

[35] Butler, "Performative Acts and Gender Constitution", 519-531; Butler, *Gender Trouble*, 79 - 149.

introduced by Scandinavian researcher Berit Ås to critique the men-women power structure in different social spaces.[36] As explained in the article *Validation Techniques and Counter Strategies: Methods for Dealing with Power Structures and Changing Social Climates,*[37] the original five techniques are as following:

Making invisible

This a common suppression technique that is used in our everyday social set up. The main point of this technique is to make someone invisible. One can do it by ignoring the person in a social setup, or by certain body language or doing activities that exclude others. One example could be that, in a corporate office space, a woman's opinion or input can be ignored. This is a suppression technique to make someone invisible from decision making.[38]

Ridiculing

Ridiculing someone or some group of people is also another typical suppression technique. For example, saying things such as, "Oh! Women are nagging all the time".[39]

Withholding Information

Withholding information is part of direct power play. Here, one party has the

---

[36] Amnéus, Diana, Eile, Ditte, Flock, Ulrika, Steuer, Pernilla Rosell & Testad, Gunnel, *Validation Techniques and Counter Strategies: Methods for Dealing with Power Structures and Changing Social Climates,* (Stockholm: Stockholm University, 2004), 2.

[37] Amnéus, Eile, Flock, Steuer, Rosell & Testad, *Validation Techniques and Counter Strategies.*

[38] Amnéus, Eile, Flock, Steuer, Rosell & Testad, *Validation Techniques and Counter Strategies,* 5.

[39] Amnéus, Eile, Flock, Steuer Rosell & Testad, *Validation Techniques and Counter Strategies,* 7.

necessary information. But, they refuse to (knowingly or unknowingly) share the information with the other party or they create situations where the other party cannot easily access this information. This introduces and maintains imbalance in power structure.[40]

Damn you if you do, damn you if you don't

This a classic technique that can put a certain group of people into confused and unsettling situation. For example, when women are commanding in workplace they might be called 'bossy' again when women are being timid and self-conscious about their actions in workplace then they might be called 'unconfident' and not fit for the workplace. It becomes, classically, "damn you if you do and damn you if you don't".[41]

Heaping blame and Putting to shame

This is a very common suppression technique that the society uses in different contexts. Through this technique, we take away voice of people and make them unconfident about their own stance. For example, when people who have faced sexual abuse speak out against the injustice done to them, then the society often blame them and put them to shame rather than questioning the unjust action and the oppressor.[42]

This research took the framework of Master Suppression Technique and widened up its possibilities to analyze the interviews to critique the power structures the participants are embedded in along with critiquing the norms associated with it.

---

[40] Amnéus, Eile, Flock, Steuer Rosell & Testad, *Validation Techniques and Counter Strategies*, 9.

[41] Amnéus, Eile, Flock, Steuer Rosell & Testad, *Validation Techniques and Counter Strategies*, 11.

[42] Amnéus, Eile, Flock, Steuer Rosell & Testad, *Validation Techniques and Counter Strategies*, 13.

"I am black, a refugee, Muslim and trans. In today's society, all of these identities are considered to be invalid. I refused to give up on my dreams and to allow society to dictate to me on what I can or can't become. Today I have a weekly blog with one of the largest papers in Malta, a monthly blog with Cambridge university, an autobiography that has launched in 6 countries, an International Peace Prize from the city of Bremen in Germany, and a young leaders award by the Queen of England. All because I refused to give up and I dared to dream big. If I can do it so can everyone else." - Farah Abdi

"Close-up: Farah Abdi," Interview, Homotropolis, published August 19, 2016, retrieved from: http://www.homotropolis.com/2016/08/news/close-up-farah-abdi/.

CHAPTER 4: METHODOLOGY

SECTION 1: FOCUS GROUP

This research focused to gather data from non-Swedish and/or non-white LGBTQIA+ students in Sweden or graduates who finished their higher education in Sweden. This focus group acted as a representative of the non-white and/or non-Swedish LGBTQIA+ people in Sweden.

SECTION 2: RECRUITING PARTICIPANTS

The project team began advertising during the autumn of 2016, with the aim of recruiting participants for the research. Firstly, a Facebook page was created to enable to reach out to the public, SFQs website got updated with information about this project and sent information to members of SFQ to reach out to SFQs own members.

Furthermore, to be able to reach out to potential participants the project team created brochures, posters and business cards containing information about the project and spread these during the autumn of 2016. These materials were sent out as digital copies together with a detailed description of the project to all the local branches of SFQ, to all the university student unions registered under SFS (Sveriges Förenade Studentkårer), to existing LGBTQIA+ organizations, and to the gender studies departments or gender studies programs at the Swedish universities. Hard copies of materials were then sent to those who showed in an interest in the project and/or interest in spreading the materials. One of the SFQ local branches in Stockholm responded to the invitation to help the project team and they have helped in spreading printed brochures and posters in the universities in Stockholm. As the project team was based in Umeå, printed brochures and posters were distributed around Umeå university area as well.

The project team and the board of SFQ have also used their networks to reach out to people. Moreover, the project team held lectures and open discussion sessions during Stockholm Pride (July 2016), Umeå Pride (September 2016), the SFQ Local Branch Conference (November 2016), and the SFQ congress (November 2016) to spread the information about the project and to be able to reach out to participants for collecting stories and conducting interviews.

Finally, the project team got in touch with nine participants. Of the nine participants that were interviewed, eight were contacted by the project team and one participant got in touch with the project team themselves when they saw the advertisement in their student union email. The project initially aimed for 12 participants for the research but it was very difficult to get in touch with people who are hidden, who are tired of talking about their experiences, or who are scared to open up about themselves. The project team followed different leads (from journalists to other LGBTQIA+ activists) to get in touch with more participants but with the concern of their safety and privacy a lot of the potential participants reported to be too scared to participate in these interviews. Therefore, it is understandable that it was not easy for people to participate in this research due to the sensitivity of the issues. However, the participants that were recruited have diversity in gender, sexuality, culture, ethnicity, status of residence permit, and the spaces they move within. The in-depth interviews with each participant gave enough data to analyze and conclude crucial results.

SECTION 3: PROFILE OF THE PARTICIPANTS

To respect the participants' anonymity, privacy and safety the identities of the participants are not disclosed. However, some background information about them that is relevant to this research and that will help the readers to connect with the book better is presented here.

The project team interviewed in total nine participants. The participants were either international and local students with non-Swedish or non-white background or students who were studying in Sweden at the time. These nine participants included students who have recently moved to Sweden and planned to stay in Sweden or who had already received permanent residency. The participants represent four different cities, and seven different schools. Since the project has a national focus, the project team aimed to recruit participants that are geographically representative of Sweden. The participants were from Umeå, Stockholm, Malmö and Gothenburg.

Among the participants there was diversity of gender (two that identify as genderqueer, one transwoman, one ciswoman, and five cismen). The participants sexuality was also diverse (two that identify as pansexual, five that identify as homosexual, and one as bisexual). Furthermore, the religious spaces (one Christian, four Muslim, three Buddhist, and one unknown) they moved within are also diverse, but among them only two were religious themselves. Five of the participants' parents were from the Middle East (as explained by the participants), of these, three are second-generation Swedish citizens and one had recently moved to Sweden. One of the participant's parents were from South East Asia and two had parents from Eastern Asia, of these, one participant was born and brought up in Sweden. One participant is from the Balkan Peninsula.

Four of the participants are second-generation Swedish citizens. Five moved to

Sweden as adults (two with a student visa, one with a partner visa, and two with permanent residency). The level of Swedish proficiency amongst the participants that had moved to Sweden as adults varied: one speaks fluent Swedish, two speak a conversational level of Swedish, one was beginning to learn Swedish at the time of the interview, and one did not speak Swedish.

SECTION 4: RESEARCH METHOD

Method 1: Online Survey

This method was used to collect personal stories from the focus group. The aim of collecting stories was to illustrate the diversity and therefore increase representation of the LGBTQIA+ community. The project team created an online questionnaire which was shared through social media. People were invited to write their stories anonymously or leave contact information for the project team. The short questionnaire asked participants to share stories that illustrated how they experience:

A. Representation within the Swedish LGBTQIA+ community and,

B. Discrimination/intolerance based on their ethnicity, culture, or religion alongside their gender identity/expression and sexuality.

The questionnaire was published in two languages: English and Swedish. The project team were also clear that survey could be translated into other languages on request. The survey used open-ended questions to encourage participants to write a descriptive story. Example questions were provided to lead the participant's stories so that they would be relevant to the project, e.g. What is it that makes you want to get involved in the LGBTQIA+ movement or activities in Sweden? Or, what it is that creates barrier to get involved? The questionnaire also asked for demographic information, including how the participant describes their cultural, ethnic and religious identity.

This method did not give any significant data that is analyzed in this book. However, one participant was recruited through this questionnaire and the stories collected were used to create graphics to share on social media.

The research analysis is based on the data gathered through Method 2: Semi-structured Interview.

Method 2: Semi-structured Interview

Semi-structured interview is a common method used method in qualitative research.[43] A semi-structured interview questionnaire was used in this project because the structure of a semi-structured interview allowed for the gathering of data in a specific framework and allowed the participants to have a flow whilst sharing their stories and experiences. The semi-structured interview was designed to help answer the questions posed by the aim of this research (how LGBTQIA+ phobia and racism are experienced and maintained within the social spaces that non-Swedish and/or non-white LGBTQIA+ people living in Sweden move within. And, to have a deeper intersectional understanding of how different levels of struggles, discriminations and violence are faced by LGBTQIA+ people who are non-white and/or non-Swedish and living in Sweden).

Based on the ideas behind performativity theory and Master Suppression Techniques (MST) the project team created a semi-structured interview protocol that would address the sense of belonging of the participants in different spaces (e.g. university, social, LGBTQIA+ organizations). This framework gave the project team data which could be analyzed to see how sense of belonging was

---

[43] Brinkmann, Svend, "Interview", in *Encyclopedia of Critical Psychology*, Teo, Thomas (ed.), (New York: Springer, 2014), 1008-1010.

related to identity construction. As well as, to consider how power structures work in the different social spaces that the participants move within. Thus, helping the project team to understand how different kinds of discrimination are experienced by the participants.

The semi-structured interview was made up of the following six sections:

1. Identity (some demographics, e.g. how would you describe your sexuality), sense of belonging (about how participants felt in different spaces together with this background and identity).

2. Social power structure in different spaces (e.g. religious space, cultural space, LGBTQIA+ space, social media, university social life, class experiences at university, family/relatives, work/study space) and its effect on identity (questions about being out or not out, financial and social independence, e.g. in what spaces are you able to express your LGBTQIA+ identity?).

3. Experiences as an LGBTQIA+ person (questions based around empowerment and safety, e.g. tell me about your positive experiences as an LGBTQIA+ person).

4. Student life (questions about study environment and experiences as a student, e.g. what do you think about your situation as a student in Sweden?).

5. Summary (about how others perceive the participant compared to how

they perceive themselves).

6. Needs (about what the participant needed to facilitate involvement in the LGBTQIA+ community, e.g. what can the community (or communities you belong to) do to empower your involvement within the LGBTQIA+ community or make you feel represented/visible in the LGBTQIA+ community in Sweden?).

The semi-structured interview created the opportunity for participants to share their unique experiences as well as give examples from specific situations. The semi-structured interview also allowed the participants to speak for themselves, as well as facilitating a friendly and accommodating environment, something that the project team valued highly. Due to the nature of semi-structured interviews, there were both positive and negative consequences for this research. The positive aspect of this was that the participants could tell their stories with flow during the interview. However, the negative aspect was that the interviewers did not comment on or challenge participant's stories during the interview which lead to the project team not to having an in-depth understanding of certain situations.

SECTION 5: DATA COLLECTION PROCESS

The interviews were, where possible, held in person. This was so that the interviewer could build rapport with the participants which would help them to feel comfortable about sharing their stories and experiences. The interviews were held by the project team. The project team conducted eight interviews in person and one interview via Skype video call (the participant was unable to meet the interviewer in person). During the interviews, the interviewer recorded the conversation (audio only). Three interviews were conducted in Swedish and the others in English. The language of the interview was decided by the participant. Each interview was 1.5 – 2.5 hours long. The recorded interviews were transcribed and all the Swedish transcripts were translated into English for the analysis. As it was a lot of data for the project team to transcribe and translate in a short time, the project team had some contributors that worked exclusively with transcribing and/or translation. The contributors signed a confidentiality agreement to protect the data and privacy of the participants.

Throughout this research the project team have had the participants' privacy and safety in mind, therefore the participants that are a part of this research are anonymous. This means that names, places and other information has been altered or withheld where needed to uphold the participant's anonymity. Participants were informed that their participation in the research was voluntary, and they were informed that interviews would be recorded and transcribed and that these files would be deleted when the research was complete. Accordingly, all recorded audio and transcripts were deleted in September 2017 upon completion of this book.

CHAPTER 5: THE QUALITATIVE ANALYSIS

The following chapters represent different themes or experiences that the project team have investigated through the interview structure and identified from the interviews. These are organized in the following way to explain and show how different layers of struggles and complexities can be experienced by different people.

To analyze the social power structure in different spaces and its effect on peoples' experiences and their identities the project team asked participants questions about their positive and negative experiences, if they can express their non-normative identity and how they are perceived in different space. As example of spaces the project included university environment, social life, digital space, personal life and so on.

The following sections follow such as: sense of belonging, student life and education, language barrier, online presence and social media. In each of these chapters the results have been analyzed from performativity theory and MSTs perspective.

SECTION 1: SENSE OF BELONGING

Through the interviews this research has observed that, the second-generation Swedish citizens grow up having an association with multiple cultures and countries. Even though they have grown up in Sweden and were therefore exposed to the normative culture in Sweden, Swedish language and Sweden their entire life, in many cases their bodies are not welcomed as stereotypical Swedish. Instead others are usually interested in knowing about their ethnic and cultural background.

This lead us to ask this question to ourselves, *"When does someone become Swedish?"* This research doesn't have any absolute answer to this question. The project concluded that, the experience of being perceived as a Swedish individual vary based on whether the person migrated to Sweden or if the person's parents or ancestors migrated to Sweden and that is judged by people by an individual's appearance and name.

White normativity in Sweden

Looking deep into the participant's experiences it became clear how a person's appearance becomes a vital factor (or a lack of factor) of being perceived as a Swedish person. This research has labeled this as white normativity in Sweden. It means that those who look closer to a stereotypical Swede, or in other words, if the person is or is perceived as white and have lighter hair color, are more likely to be assumed as a Swedish person. Moreover, a person's name also plays a vital role in this norm. Based on the interviews, it became clear that it rarely matters if the person considers themselves Swedish or if the person considers themselves belonging to Sweden, since the power structures in society are always there to judge a person's *Swedishness* based on what they look like and what their name is. This means a person's appearance (skin-hair color) and name are the two vital signs that associates with one's identity as a Swedish person. This fits well with Butler's performativity theory where different bodies are perceived based on normative expectations.[44]

In this context, the second-generation Swedish participants who claimed to have their sense of belonging towards Sweden, are often not considered *Swedish*. Due to the power structure in the Swedish society, where whiteness is the norm they are often positioned as non-Swedish. This has been the experience of all the participants who are second-generation Swedish citizens: they are often not considered as a Swedish person. This also reflects the problematization of the term 'Second-generation Swedish' citizens.

Interestingly, one of the participants who is viewed as a white person expressed a similar perspective that people would assume that they are Swedish or *European* whereas they moved to Sweden very recently. This participant said:

> "When they do not interact with me... when they see me in the street... they see me as... I don't know half-blonde Swedish... The way I look, it (goes with) European so they do not assume on the first glance, that I am (an) immigrant. This is shallow but this is my experience. I will say so. Like they will ask me things in Swedish... Like also, right now I am thinking of the different contexts I have been.'"

This reaffirmed the concept of white normativity in the identity formation in

---

[44] Butler, "Performative Acts and Gender Constitution", 519-531; Butler, *Gender Trouble*.

Sweden. If someone looks normatively white and have stereotypical *Swedish* looks then they may appear to be a Swedish person in the Swedish community. However, if the person fails to appear white, then no matter whether they are born and brought up here, they will most likely be considered as a non-Swedish person.

Another aspect of sense of belonging is how this changes as a body moves through different spaces. Here are some examples of how others' interpretations of the participants changed when they were outside of Sweden, and how this is related to, and influences, even their sense of belonging in Sweden.

One of the participant's that was a second-generation Swedish citizen noticed that when they travel abroad, their *Swedishness* is accepted, even though it isn't accepted when they are in Sweden:

> "But when I'm in abroad – there were people who asked, and then I said Sweden. And people treated it like it was normal. So, Yes. I don't view it in the way that you can say fifty-fifty, but I view it more as I am one hundred percent Swedish and one hundred percent *XYZ*."

Interestingly, some other participants expressed similar experience, when they travelled abroad and they were perceived as Swedish. Most interestingly, one participant shared their experience visiting their parents' home country. There they were perceived as an outsider - a *'Westerner'* - a *'Swede'* visiting who does not have enough cultural association and contextual knowledge related to that country. Another participant (who came to Sweden recently and holds a permanent residency) had very similar experience. This participant added:

"When I went to Y country, I was in that power position. In Y country, I was for them, a (person) from Sweden. Because, I was living in Sweden. But, I was explaining to them overtime (that), I am from X country, this is my X country's passport, and I am one of you. But for them (people from Y country), I was whiter than them, and here (in Sweden), I am X country person. I am a victim, and people want to help me or to rescue me. After they make sure that, I am not a terrorist (laughter). But, there (in Y country) I was a white foreigner. There, they wanted to take photo with me all the time. So, I was there (at the beach) with a girl from Australia, she was originally from Finland, very white, and blonde hair. In the beach, there were some boys (who) ran to me, they wanted to take photos with me'. I was always trying to avoid that situation, but at the same time, I couldn't speak with them, it was hard to explain that, I don't want to take photo with you but it doesn't mean I don't respect. But then they saw that Australian girl, and all of them left me, they ran to her, they took photos with her. I was like, okay, we don't need to have photo, it was such a relief, at the same time it was so funny that, I was not enough of a white foreigner (compared to other person). I was a white foreigner as long as there was not a better representative (laughter). (laughter)."

Here, it can be seen, how our performances and which spaces we are associated with gives a perception about us. Extending Butler's theory,[45] it can be seen that, in a white normative Swedish space, some may pass as a Swedish person whilst some might not, based on their appearance and their names. Again, those who are not passing as a Swede and/or a Swedish person, might be perceived as a Swedish person when they are in another culture (in other spaces). That means that the same body is perceived as a Swedish person and not as a Swedish person

---

[45] Butler, "Performative Acts and Gender Constitution", 519-531; Butler, *Gender Trouble*, 79-149.

in different spaces based on what association that space has with *Swedishness*. For example: In the example given above, those people in Indonesia who were trying to take photos with this participant perceived the participant as a white Swedish person because the participant was perceived *whiter* than other people there and the participant was living in Sweden. But, the same person again does not have enough physical similarities with the stereotypical Swedish people to be considered as a Swedish person in Sweden.

Layers of complexities in sense of belonging

During conversations with the participants of Making Space, the project team found a similarity among many of the participants: complexities of being a part of several intimate cultures. They sometimes struggle with their associations with different cultures again they cherish what they have. Each cultural association brings a different layer in their identity and their experiences. Sometimes, they view them a part of all the cultures again sometimes they view them part of no culture.

For example, when asked about their cultural belonging one participant (second-generation Swedish citizen) expressed the struggle of being part of the dominant culture in Sweden but again not having enough association with or information about Swedish pop-culture or tradition:

> "(Culturally) I will go with Swedish but with a twist on it. Because I can understand when I am with my Swedish friends they know a lot more about Swedish, pop-culture... I think it is... like celebrities and like old (Swedish) celebrities that their parents, when they were children, they watched. (They watched) Swedish television but we didn't (do) that in our house."

This research also came across people who are struggling to be part of different cultures as part of their identity. Especially one of the participants who recently moved to Sweden from a Middle Eastern country felt an outsider from both Swedish and Middle Eastern community, again confused if they could be in-between these two cultures, or a mix of two. Or, just outside of it all trying to find a space where they would fit being a homosexual Middle Eastern Swedish person?

"The biggest thing is that I am gonna try to defend the Middle-eastern culture in front of them (the Swedes) and then when it comes to me saying that I am homosexual, all my good ideas that I could say about (my culture), that gonna be totally misunderstood or misrepresented if I'd compare to me being a homosexual person in the Middle-east and how scary it is to be LGBT there. So, I feel like I try to defend (a) culture that doesn't accept me as a homosexual person but accept me like (a Middle Eastern). I like it (Sweden) who accepts me as a homosexual person but (again it) doesn't accept me as (a) Middle-eastern."

This participant elaborates their complex connection with their extended family and friends from their Middle Eastern association:

"I have a really good connection with them (Middle Eastern friends and family). But, I feel I am left out... because most of them are either have long-term relationships or they are already engaged. And everyone like just asking me why I don't have any partner...

My uncle; he always talks openly about him being disgusted by gay people. It's really harsh to hear your uncle like I have a really good relationship with him. He loves me and he sees like big deal of me but in me...

(On the other hand) The Middle-eastern or immigrant community gay guys (in Sweden) that I talk to. Most of them are either in denial still or they can't see themselves out to their family, at all. (It's) like they could live their lives inside the closet (forever). And I can't understand them as well because like here in Sweden you have a really good network of protection and social reliance you could use. Me being from Middle East, I could see the big differences between the two countries (Sweden and the country he is from). That I could take advantage of the positive things that here that are here in Sweden. I am just more open-minded (now). But ya, that's the problem, with the Swedes that they see it weird not being out and for the Middle-Easterns (I know), they see it weird being out."

Most of the participants who are born and brought up in Sweden have very strong cultural and social connection with Sweden which leads them to build their identity around Sweden. However, as their parents have social ties and/or belonging in another country and/or culture, some of them also feel strongly connected with their parent's country or culture. This was true for some participants, who either defined themselves as being 'in-between' different cultures, or as being '100%' in all the belonging cultures.

"Yes, there is some kind of feeling of being in-between... Because you are both like Vietnamese and Swedish, so sometimes you have to... put weight on certain parts, because it is impossible to... know everything about like – what it means to be totally Swedish and totally Vietnamese as well. Then you feel some kind of feeling of being in-between." - Said one participant

Another participant explains how the question "where are you from?" reminds them of this complexity:

> "It is enough that someone asks, 'where are you from?' I will directly be like 'Oh, shit. What am I going to answer?' A thousand thoughts come to me. Like, what does the question mean?"

Another participant added to this context:

> "When I'm in Sweden and talk about nationality, it's like (my nationality) spontaneously becomes XYZ (where his parents are from). Because most people (here in Sweden) who ask about (my) nationality clearly mean my external. That's what they see. I do not think anyone asks anyone white "What nationality are you?" when they speak Swedish with each other. So that's why I always respond like, 'Yes, my parents are from XYZ but I was born in Sweden'.

There were also participants who felt that they belonged nowhere, and instead described a feeling out being an outsider both here in Sweden and in their parent's culture.

> "Yes, so it is... It is a kind of feeling of being in between. It is... Sometimes you are both and sometimes you are neither."
> – Said one participant.

Overall, this section shows how people's perception about Swedish identity makes the second-generation Swedish citizens feel alienated in the land where they were born and brought up. From the perspective of the MST theory this is an example of the MST "making invisible," where a person is made invisible by the people in power. This section also elaborates the layers of complexities around the sense of belonging towards Sweden and other cultures that non-white and/or non-Swedish people are part of. Moreover, the participants that have migrated to Sweden, in one way or another expressed that they don't want to live in their country of origin even though some of them have strong emotional and social connection with their country because their gender identity and/or expression and/or their sexuality and/or sexual orientation is not as accepted in their home country. These people see Sweden as a more vibrant country in terms of LGBTQIA+ rights than many other countries and their home countries. Among them some want to carry their cultural and religious heritage with them and again some just want to create their own cultural and social identity in Sweden. Most of them are trying to integrate into Swedish society by, for example learning Swedish and trying pass as a Swedish person. They only hope that the Swedish society would embrace them with time.

SECTION 2: LANGUAGE BARRIER

When people are situated and move within different spaces where knowing a specific language is a norm then that structure itself creates and maintains a power hierarchy within the people who know that language and who don't. Even though if two people are in the same space for example at a discussion session held in Swedish, if one person does not know Swedish then it puts the person who doesn't know Swedish experiencing the same space differently than the other person. Among the participants who are international students this issue of language barrier was very common. Specially, if they were not already associated with LGBTQIA+ activism, it was difficult for them to know what kinds of LGBTQIA+ organizations that are working in Sweden. The project identified that, it created another level of power hierarchy among the participants.

One participant talked about how they felt left out in a social platform aimed at students and locals at their university because they could not speak Swedish, even though the platform mentioned in the example is an open innovation platform which is open for everyone:

> "Yeah (there is) a place[46] (in our university campus) for people to go there to make something like... there's some 3D printer or there's a cutter, located at the Art campus. But there everyone talks in Swedish, so it's really, I think it's really hard to get involved in any kind of group in Sweden if I don't speak Swedish."

---

[46] An open innovation platform where anyone can stop by, use the materials available, and socialize.

They also mentioned about how it was difficult for them to interpret their housing contracts and bank information:

> "Some kinds of information are in Swedish only. And, yes, it's not easy for foreigners, to know everything here... Ah... The contract of house or the contract of phone... or even internet... And, sometimes you have to contact the person, contact the company, and you dial a phone number. And... the answer machine is all in Swedish. And, yes, sometimes you have to try a lot, or wait for a long time."

These experiences show another layer of struggle that newcomers students go through in their everyday life while maintaining their studies and lives in Sweden.

The international students reported during the interview that, their educational institutions are aware of the students who don't speak Swedish. Therefore, the universities try to provide the new students with necessary information such as: where or how to get housing, where to access health care and so on. However, these participants reported that they were not introduced to any LGBTQIA+ organizations by their university and they rarely found information about LGBTQIA+ issues and rights in Sweden. This illustrates a power structure in which Swedish speakers have easier access to resources than their non-Swedish speaking counterparts.

Again, in the similar context, the experiences of the participants who were already involved in LGBTQIA+ activism in other countries was different. In case of these participants not knowing Swedish did not create that much of a barrier in terms of getting information as they already knew where or how to find the information related to LGBTQIA+ activism or organization working in Sweden. Another of the participants stated that it was her trans-identity within her gender studies class gave her more power to critique gender and the same time her being in the gender studies class made her feel safe about her identity:

> "Everything is great. You have a transgender person at gender studies which implicitly make me a queen of gender studies. And everything is just great like from the instructors, professors and other students that that are like so much into gender studies...I really feel loved by my friends and I love them so much. And I really, I told you this is like literally the happiest part of my life. Just because it's peaceful and normal, I am living in a space and I am really happy."

In case of people who are already exposed to LGBTQIA+ activism and/or LGBTQIA+ community had higher power than the ones who don't. They knew where to look for information or how to get involved in LGBTQIA+ activism in Sweden or had the tools to feel safe with their LGBTQIA+ identities. This intersectionality of knowing-not knowing Swedish and having-not having access to LGBTQIA+ activism shows a variance in the power structure of the spaces the non-white and/or non-Swedish LGBTQIA+ people move within.

In the context of language barrier, one participant reported that when they tried to find out information about LGBTQIA+ organizations in Sweden, they could not get enough information. Moreover, he did not even know about SFQ beforehand. When asked what search engine did they use they replied that they used Google. To understand the situation better the project conducted a controlled experiment. The team searched on Google (www.google.se)

anonymously[47] with the LGBTQIA+ related common keywords and analyzed the results obtained from the search. The project team considered only searching on Google because that's the search engine the participants used and this is the most popular search engine used in Sweden.[48]

The project team searched the keywords: *'LGBT Sweden'*, *'LGBT organization Sweden'*, *'Gay Lesbian Sweden'*, and *'Transgender Sweden'* and received the following research results which included 'RFSL' as the most popular result. Other organizations like SFQ, Transföreningen FPES or Transammans did not come up in the search results.

---

[47] When searching online through Google, it usually shows a customized search result mainly based on the keyword searched, location of the device (where we are searching from), and previous search history. They also have other advertisement policies on what search results pop up first. To ensure that our previous search history did not influence these searches the project team used the 'incognito' feature of Mozilla browser which ensured anonymity.

[48] "Search Engine Market Share in Sweden, August 2016 - August 2017" Statcounter Global Stats, accessed September 9, 2017, http://gs.statcounter.com/search-engine-market-share/all/sweden.

Search Keyword: LGBT Sweden
(Last retrieved June 1 2017)

Search keyword: LGBT organisations Sweden (Last retrieved June 1 2017)

Search keyword: Gay Lesbian organisations Sweden (Last retrieved June 1 2017)

Search keyword: Transgender organisations Sweden (last retrieved June 1 2017)

To see how easy it is to find out on Google what LGBTQIA+ organizations are working in Sweden, the project team searched with keywords: 'List of LGBT organizations in Sweden'. The results included: a list of all LGBTQIA+ organization in the world published in *Wikipedia*,[49] and a list of the organizations in Sweden[50] (in English) published at a Swedish government agency, *Information om Sverige*, website. On the *Wikipedia* page under Sweden only 'The Ombudsman against Discrimination on Grounds of Sexual Orientation (government office)' and 'RFSL' were listed (last retrieved June 1, 2017). The list on *Information om Sverige* contained a list of many organizations and links to their websites. However, it was not mentioned which organizations are LGBTQIA+ organizations (last retrieved June 1, 2017).

Search keyword: List of LGBT organisations in Sweden (Last retrieved June 1 2017)

---

[49] "List of LGBT Rights Organisations", Wikipedia, accessed June 1, 2017,
https://en.wikipedia.org/wiki/List_of_LGBT_rights_organisations.
[50] "Associations and organisations", Information om Sverige, accessed June 1, 2017,
http://www.informationsverige.se/Engelska/Leva-och-bo/Foreningar-och-organisationer/Pages/Start.aspx.

This further shows the difficulty of finding LGBTQIA+ organizations that work in Sweden, when searching with Google in English. However, the project team acknowledge that many LGBTQIA+ organizations are including information in English on their websites, but when searched on Google not everything came up. Therefore, a list of LGBTQIA+ organizations in Sweden is presented at the end of this book.

During the interviews of Making Space, most participants that were new to Sweden also mentioned that most of the LGBTQIA+ events on Facebook, along with some other events aimed at students or others, only had the descriptions in Swedish. This makes it difficult to understand what the event is about and it also makes them feel unwelcome. On top of that, there has also been situations where not knowing Swedish makes someone out of the space sometimes. These are regular life experience of international students studying in Sweden.

What this research have identified through these interviews and this controlled experiment is that information and resources which are only available in Swedish create a language barrier, which makes it very difficult for non-Swedish speakers to access basic information on the LGBTQIA+ community and rights in Sweden. This can be understood from the MST of withholding information. In a system where information is only available in Swedish, the system therein creates a power structure that indirectly withholds information from those without access to the Swedish language whilst at the same time it makes non-Swedish speakers invisible. This research also shows that overall language barrier works as an extra layer of struggle for LGBTQIA+ people that are new to Sweden and/or do not speak Swedish.

To cope with the language barrier most of the participants reported to be studying Swedish. However, this research acknowledges that, it requires extra time and energy from newcomers to manage their regular studies, work, activities, as well as learning Swedish. In this situation, they require support from their university association and other communities.

SECTION 3: STUDENT LIFE AND THE EDUCATION ENVIRONMENT

Seven of the participants had experience from university, whilst two participants only had experienced other adult education forms in Sweden. These adult education forms were: SFI (Swedish for immigrants), Komvux (adult education) and Folk High School (adult education, generally at high-school level or courses for specific occupations). The concepts of both student life and the academic environment can be viewed as a space that these participants move within. For this research, student life means the specific combination of social expectations, economic resources, and status in society that students in higher education have.

Power hierarchy based on access to CSN

Two of the participants with permanent residency who had come to Sweden recently were able to receive the same opportunities in terms of education as a Swedish citizen. For example, education was free for them and they received CSN (Swedish government's financial aid for studying) to support themselves during their study period. As they came to Sweden from other countries that do not have free education and the system of CSN, they were able to acknowledge how that has helped them to become independent and in turn made them psychologically and financially more stable. This new independence allowed them to begin the process of coming out. Access to CSN is one example of power which influences expressing someone's LGBTQIA+ which can be seen from Butler's performativity theory[51] that talks about performing in a certain way in certain spaces. There is a hierarchy of those that have CSN and those that do not have CSN. Therefore, the

---

[51] Butler, "Performative Acts and Gender Constitution", 519-531; Butler, *Gender Trouble*, 79-149.

research has shown from the lens of performativity theory that an individual's position on this hierarchy influences therefore how they perform. The individual's behavior in this case, choosing to come out, is shaped based on the power they hold. Whereas, those participants who are second-generation Swedish citizens did not take up issues of free education and CSN. This goes back to performativity theory because different groups of people perform in different ways, even within the same space, based on what power they have. The project team sees that this was the case because for a person who has grown up in Sweden it is more common that these opportunities are normalized. From this understanding, it is assumed that, many Swedish citizens might not actually realize the privileges they hold compared to many other newcomers.

> "That's a good thing with Sweden because it's easy to be financially independent. It's (a) way to for you to be financially independent especially when you are a student... I have a student loan (CSN). I live by myself now. So, I have like the freedom of being out as everyone."
> - Said one participant

Cis-heteronormativity and white-normativity in educational environments

In Sweden, every educational institute in Sweden must write and follow a plan for equal opportunities (likabehandlingsplan in Swedish) as well as have an action plan about how to process violations of this plan. These policy documents act as a guide for reducing harassment and discrimination in the education environment as well as regulating how students and staff can complain if they feel discriminated against or harassed based on, for example, skin color, religion, or sexuality.

However, in practice, is the picture so bright and shiny? As mentioned earlier in this book, SFQ has already shown in Avslöja heteronormen! that many of these plans lack a norm critical, intersectional, perspective of people's identities and sexualities. Although an analysis of these policy documents isn't a part of the present project, here are some relevant findings from the interviews that show examples of when young LGBTQIA+ students haven't received the support they deserve from their universities or schools.

During the interviews, it came out that some of the participants are subjected to white normativity and racism in academic environments. Moreover, because of the participants' non-normative gender identity and/expression and/or their sexuality and/sexual orientation, they are also subjected cis-heteronormativity, LGBTQIA+ phobia. The participants have described the intersection amongst different forms of racism, discrimination, and norms that they have experienced during their time in education in Sweden.

Cis-heteronormativity

The participants shared stories of how the normative student environment made them feel left out in different ways. These two following quotes are examples from two participants stories. The first quote describes how absence of a space for LGBT students at university made this participant feel lonely. The second quote is an illustration of how student events uphold cis- and heteronormativity, this is problematic for LGBTQIA+ students because many do not feel included in cis- heteronormative environments.

"It's been very lonely (at university). I don't think there is any LGBT club or something like that in the school. I am the only gay person I know of... No, I don't really feel like there is any place for like LGBT people. It's not I want to exclude people. But, there is no place to talk about it... like LGBT people." – Said one participant

"Stuff happens that I feel is problematic... there are various themed dinners and... there is the... 'macho-sitting', and where it's... just guys who can join, and what you do before you go to dinner is to, like, do typical macho stuff... So, you roll big tires and such... Competitions... You're just "what?". While the girls go on... a girl-dinner and then it is like fine dining. They sit together and ... Yes, you know it's very much like that." – Said one participant

Furthermore, one participant that was studying medicine explained that they were subject to homophobia by a fellow classmate, they give examples here:

"He (a classmate) said 'are you gay because you like being gay?' And I was really struck because like this person is gonna be a doctor here (in Sweden) and people or children are gonna come to him and gonna say to him like 'I feel different'... I don't know (what) his reply is gonna be. He always tries to convince me that men... are cleverer than women, like genetically. He always tries to convince me and the others... He says, 'I like you even though you are gay, because you don't seem like a gay.'"

Even with the positive exeriences within the classroom and program, this participant unfortunately had experiences of discrimination outside of the classroom. In the quote below, she explains how another student looked her up and down and said, "what the fuck," presumably based on the her non-normative, trans, body:

> "He came towards me and like looked at me like from the head to the toes and just said like 'What the fuck?' And made kind of face that of like disgust about me... of course it is truly (about my) transgender identity."

Other participant's shared similar experiences from people studying in different disciplines in the universities that not always their classmates are aware of the cis-heteronormativity and are not always sensitive towards LGBTQIA+ issues.

One participant tried to illustrate the way in which one's own needs or experience is made invisible by the LGBTQIA+ community not being explicit about the expectations and norms within the group. Participants reported that they knew about a local branch of SFQ or other LGBTQIA+ student group, but that they couldn't or hadn't joined because they were afraid that they would be outed. Below is a quote which demonstrates how not specifically stating that your organization or group is a safe space for all students, even if you are not out or have a hidden identity. This participant explained that he assumed all board members and active members of his local LGBTQIA+ student group had to be public about their LGBTQIA+ identity.

> "It's hard to be involved in the LGBTQ community because as I said I feel that they are waiting from you to be open to all people in your life or like most people of your life. So, for me it feels hard to be like an active individual there because of me being not open. I feel that, that's a limitation for me. And they don't say that openly but like every activity they have or every opportunity they have, it has like its demands

for you, for me, to be open to everyone that I know and I can't be open right now. So, ya, that's a limitation I think."

These experiences from the participants also show why there is a need for local groups for students. This is important so that they can find a community of other LGBTQIA+ people, who share similar experiences of facing cis-heteronormativity in the normative student environment. These experiences also show that the activists and volunteers working in the local branches who have direct contact with the students themselves need to be constantly updated with knowledge on diversity and inclusiveness in the community. Local branches of SFQ and other local LGBTQIA+ groups can also act as a place of education, where members can learn more about the diversity within the community and how to be inclusive, learn from one another's experiences and share stories. However, LGBTQIA+ groups should never be a place where racism or other oppression (for example, based on gender, ability, age, or religion) are accepted.

The participants have shared negative stories about SFI (Swedish for immigrants) from two different cities. This shows that SFI is not always successful in creating safer space for LGBTQIA+ people and that cis-heteronormativity exists at SFI as well. The following quote shows one of the participants' experience at SFI:

"The boss (counsellor) of SFI (he asked me why I came here, and I said to him) 'oh I come with my boyfriend', and he said, 'next time you can say, I come with my family'. So, I feel, is it impacting you or something.... I thought it's quite common (to be a gay man in Sweden) but I took a step back and reconsidered that."

The issue with this participant's experience lies with the fact that a person in a position of power, such as a coordinator or director of a program, or a teacher or counsellor in SFI, at universities or schools, have a lot of power and influence through their position.

Another participant expressed their struggles of fighting the cis-heteronormativity in SFI and at the end not being able to continue at SFI:

> "I had the feeling that they (my classmates) wanted to control me in the same way the Middle-Eastern traditional society wanted to control me (when I was back in home). And, it was one of the reason that, at the end, I was not interested in continuing learning Swedish. I had that social pressure on myself that, I had this feeling I need to censor myself. I could write in… for example… my essay… for my teacher that I was into Pride, but I couldn't talk about it publicly in the school (SFI)."

SFI is a very important space where most newcomers end up in their first years in Sweden (to be able to learn Swedish). Those that work with people who are new to Sweden have a lot of power to be able to empower LGBTQIA+ newcomers, and to question cis-heteronormativity in the educational environment and to educate their students on LGBTQIA+ issues alongside of their subject's curriculum. But, for example, telling a person who has recently arrived in Sweden that they should keep their same-sex relationship hidden, makes their non-heteronormative identity invisible. These kinds of power plays reinforce cis-heteronormativity, give a feeling of shame, guilt or unsafety, and a feeling of, "I don't belong here", which can have a big impact on those who are new to Sweden. Form Butler's theory, it can be said that, this cis-heteronormative power structure at SFI influences the non-white and/or non-Swedish

LGBTQIA+ students to censor their identity and perform in a certain way that fits the normative expectations which the space puts upon them to be able to get through their education.[52]

Bi-invisibility in the Swedish LGBTQIA+ community and in student community, was another point that came up during the interviews. Even in gender studies courses this participant did not find enough bi-inclusiveness. The following quote shows the lack of bi-inclusivity even within the people who focus on LGBTQIA+ questions:

> "There was a Swedish guy there who was writing his thesis (about LGBTQ). He asked me to be part of his research. And then, I said, yah, 'I have already had so many interviews with people in... (here). So, you can ask someone else.' Then he said, 'But, you can you can be the L in my research'. Then I said, 'I am sorry but I am not the L.' Then he said, 'I am sorry I thought you are a lesbian. So, are you heterosexual?' Then I said, 'Noo!' Then, he didn't know what I am. Like, he was confused!"

See more about bi-invisibility in *Chapter 9: Bi invisibility in Sweden and academia: from the perspective of an Iranian activist.*

White normativity and racism

One of the participants experienced a lot of marginalization in their learning environment, which was as part of a program at a Folk High School. These experiences of belittling and exclusion, and at times violent harassment, led the

---

[52] Butler, "Performative Acts and Gender Constitution", 519-531; Butler, *Gender Trouble*, 79- 149.

participant to rethink their plans of studying further. During the interview the participant explained that they couldn't consider studying further being placed in an environment with people who express racism and LGBTQIA+ phobia. Because, they were unable to cope with being forced into working together with people who oppress them.

> "It (the program) was extremely white... and experiences there, is from LGBTQ people as well as, white LGBTQ people subjected me to a lot of marginalization and racism. So, experiences there have led up to me not being able to cope with living a student life that forces me into group work and relationships that I don't decide for myself."

This same participant had complained to the staff about these negative experiences of intolerance and racism in the classroom, and was met with critique and denial instead of support.

> "I experienced racism, I did. There are others than me now that also (experience racism), and... there's no one who does anything... all the teachers, the whole staff is white so they don't have any experience or knowledge about racism. It's a lot of... what should I call it, (they said to me) 'it is this your subjective experience...' Making you, making you believe that what happened never took place and that you yourself are sort of... that it's your problem, the problem is with you"

Through this critique and denial, the group who holds the power through their authoritative position and white normativity make the experiences, struggles, and discrimination of someone with less power as a non-white student invalid.

Therefore, their voices are made invisible, this is an example of the MST "making invisible". The research has shown from the interviews that this is a common experience for marginalized groups.

This experience also shows that Master suppression techniques such as "heaping blame" and "damn if you do, damn if you don't" takes place in the academic environments in Sweden. When an individual faces racism and complain about it, then they get judged that they are complaining all the time. Again, it is heard many times that, if there is racism in Sweden, where are the stories or where is the proof? The interviews showed that, when people keep facing discrimination for a very long time, sometimes they get tired of being the one complaining about it and not being able to change the situation.

This leads to people feeling powerless and not complaining. Another participant shares a story below about the difference experiences as a person of color from growing up in a diverse neighborhood, to changing schools, and starting university. They share unfortunately that they now have an extreme atmosphere in their university class, which has led to them needing to *"tone themselves down"* or self-censor them so that they do not have to engage in verbal conflict with class members.

"For the first few years, I started in the immigrants settled area and it was a lot of fun. Everybody coming from all over the world. It wasn't really you are the only one... Since we moved, we were (the) new guys, and, right now in white suburb area, I only had one friend, this Pakistani girl and her family. But, the school, it was terrible, I hated it. I was bullied, they didn't know I was gay. I was like 15 or 16... it was mostly racially motivated... (Then) my high school... all three years were absolutely marvelous... My niche (in the high school) was this leftie LGBT place, (there wasn't) a lot of LGBT (people) of color but at least it felt safe in terms of being different... Then when I started university, I (realized), not everyone actually feels the same as you do... And I guess that was a bummer. It wasn't too unexpected but then again, my class (has a) quite extreme atmosphere. I have some very top-notch Nazi liberals in my class. So, I have come to verbal conflict with some of them... Right now, I feel like it's pretty calm. I don't (engage myself in verbal conflicts) ... I have toned down myself."

This whole discourse and power structure of: not getting enough support when complaining about the struggles and discrimination you face, getting drained of energy from fighting to be heard, and toning oneself down, is one of the ways in that the power structure where non-white and/or non-Swedish LGBTQIA+ people face struggles and discrimination is maintained.

SECTION 4: LIFE IN DIGITAL SPACE

During the interviews participants experiences in digital-social spaces came up intensively. The research identified that the cis-heteronormative and white normative structure the participants are struggling with in their regular life is also present in their digital space. Therefore, in this section the participant's experiences using social media is analyzed. The analysis is presented under the following themes: Body politics and White Normativity, Safety and Privacy, Hatred in Social Media, and Social Media: A space for activism.

Body politics and White Normativity

The first section of this chapter discussed the prevalence of white normativity in terms of perceiving Swedish identities. This segment elaborates the prevalence of similar situations in the digital space. When asked about their experiences in social media several participants brought up their experiences on dating applications.

On social media people usually represent themselves through texts, pictures, and sometimes videos. What people describe about themselves and what people share on social media becomes a part of how they express their identity. This is especially important on dating applications such as Tinder and Grindr. There is only a few photos and a few words (i.e.: name and biography) about a person that reflects an image of the person's identity. Which leads others to perceive that image from their own perspective.

All the participants who are second-generation Swedish citizens and who mentioned about Tinder and Grindr during the interviews expressed how narrowly their image is perceived and judged by a portion of the white Swedish community. Even though their social media profile reflects that they speak Swedish and that they are from Sweden.

One of the participants shared their frustration during their interview:

> "They (white Swedes) usually assume that I am (a) foreigner and I can't speak Swedish. It's pretty common... Let me give (you) an example. If you are using Grindr. People would rather write to me in English and wouldn't take the time to read one sentence in my profile that (says that) I am Swedish or (they wouldn't) actually get that I speak Swedish. I don't usually reply to those. Cause it means that, you (they) kind of have a weird mindset. You might have even read the profile. It's (the profile introduction description) not even more than 140 characters. So, it's not like thinking more than two minutes."

This experience shows that, people tend to decide if someone is a Swedish person based on the person's picture and names, or in other words, based on if the person has stereotypical white Swedish attributes and name. Therefore, the non-normative bodies that don't live up to the expectations of white-normativity fail to pass as a Swedish person even on social media. This can be again viewed from Butler's theory,[53] which states that based on certain norms a person's identity gets judged and perceived by others. In this research, the participants' image on social media failed to be perceived as the image of a "Swedish person".

---

[53] Butler, "Performative Acts and Gender Constitution", 519-531; Butler, *Gender Trouble*, 79-149.

Ahmed, 32
Anders har skickat ett meddelande?

Anders, 26

Heya? You make me think about 1000 £ a night... Wanna be my alladin? ;)
Haha... Aldrig gillat rollspel :p

Åh, du kan svenska? Du skriver rätt bra, hur länge har du bott i Sverige? :)
Sedan jag föddes här!...

Interestingly, the image of a person's identity in social media that fails to be perceived as a Swedish person, is also, in many cases, subject to exotification. This issue was brought up in some interviews with the participants. For example: one participant explained their experience of being in the gay community on Grindr and Tinder:

> "They just (talk) about my hair and that it's so exotic and exciting and... I don't know... but I can sometimes feel as like, ah exotified basically... As if I'm a... product."

However, these experiences of exotification are unfortunately not exclusive to social media and the internet. The participants reflected on similar experiences in real life as well as virtual experiences.

Another issue that one of the participant's highlighted in the interviews was that some bodies are excluded in gay dating culture in Sweden based on the racialization of some *ethnic* features. For example, the participant expressed how on the dating applications many people write '*no Asians*', or similar racist phrases.

> "It can be seen very clear in (the) dating apps where it is very clear that many write in their profile that they are not looking for Asians. Uh, and it's – it makes you very sad because one is not just Asian. Eh... (Laughter) What is it you are looking for? It is, yes – when you ask, "What is it you do not see in an Asian?" so people usually always come up the stereotypical picture. I mean, then they always explain very stereotypical. Which is racism. So, it ... Which means that in the LGBTQ world, it is extremely normalized that it's okay to be this racist, because of the fact that they are oppressed in a different way. But just because you are oppressed in one

a way so does not mean that that justifies even racism as
well."

Therefore, besides exotification, there are experiences of *exclusion and ridiculing* in the social media culture. People's ethnicity becomes the standard of their existence in the dating culture in the digital world (social media). These experiences are also extensions of MST making invisible and MST ridiculing.

These examples sum up the body politics on social media that the non-white LGBTQIA+ people face. Their bodies are sometimes excluded from the white-Swedish normative structure, sometimes exotified again sometimes ridiculed and excluded.

Safety and Privacy

This segment presents how social media had an impact on the participant's safety and privacy. This section addresses the most popular social media platform used in Sweden: Facebook.[54] This is because the participants shared their experiences using Facebook.

The project team has seen that LGBTQIA+ organizations in Sweden use Facebook pages alongside other mediums to share information with the public.

---

[54] "Facebook Dominates and Twitter Drops – How Swedes Use Social Media", The Internet Foundation in Sweden, October 13, 2016,
https://www.iis.se/english/press/pressreleases/facebook-dominates-and-twitter-drops-how-swedes-use-social-media-2016/.

On Facebook pages, organizations post information and create events. Even though Facebook is widely used, Facebook itself has specific mechanisms that control the accessibility of such Facebook events and information shared on Facebook from specific Facebook profiles (this is explained further below). This research has seen that, these mechanisms can directly and indirectly affect an individual's safety and privacy. This research identified that, in case of *hidden identities on social media,* these mechanisms impose a great impact which is not always considered.

What is meant by *hidden identities on social media and* what is meant by *mechanism in Facebook?* For this research, Hidden identities on social media, are the LGBTQIA+ people who did not or could not yet come out as a LGBTQIA+ person on their social media and/or their regular life, and in most cases, they hide the fact that they have any affiliation with LGBTQIA+ issues, rights, or events/activities on social media. This book introduced this concept earlier in this chapter, under section 3. Here it will be elaborated in the context of social media. Two of the nine interviewees are hidden identities on social media. For two other participants, it was not completely black or white. They reported that they can be open about themselves on social media, but that they need to be careful about their privacy settings.

The popular mechanisms in Facebook are: like, share, comment and accessing public information or friends' information. In the case of the hidden identities, they cannot like or follow the LGBTQIA+ organizations on Facebook. The reason behind this is how these mechanisms influence how information are flowing on Facebook. If someone likes a page or a post on Facebook, then that can appear as a post on the *newsfeed* (knows as 'Home') of Facebook of their most interacted 'friends' or of their 'friends of friends' (both web and app version). Moreover, on the web version, it may appear randomly on the left bar (referred

to as the *'Ticker'* by Facebook) of Facebook as a continuous thread on their friends'
and/or friends of friends' homepage. 'Ticker' is a function that allows people to
view what their friends are posting, liking, or sharing in real time.[55]

There is another feature on Facebook called groups. In terms of Facebook groups,
there are three types of privacy settings: Public (the group is open to all), closed
(the group is open to only members approved by the admin or other members
and you can see the group and its members even if you are not a member), and
secret (you cannot see the group, cannot join the group if you are not added by an
Admin or other members). That means, that if a hidden identity joins a public or
closed LGBTQIA+ group on Facebook, others will be able to see it. One of the
participants shared their experience of this with us:

> "I cannot write openly about my experiences being gay (and)
> about difficulties being gay in Middle-eastern community. I
> cannot like pages (or show) I could be interested or go to
> events that are (related to) gay (community) or something
> (like that) on Facebook. So, that's (being able to share) for
> me... that's being out on social media. And I don't do that at
> all, obviously! It feels frustrating! Really frustrating! ... It
> takes its toll on you, on your daily life, especially on social
> media and when I started going out to gay clubs and gay bars
> with my friends and it's really frustrating for them to just
> mention it casually on social media and for me just being on,
> in the background! ... It takes its toll. But you get used to it
> and when you see a lot of other people, that have the same
> problem as you... You see, it... it becomes easier."

These situations can make it impossible for hidden identities to be able to even
follow the news and activities/events related to LGBTQIA+ issues on social

---

media. Whereas, among the participants who do not have hidden identities activities on Facebook are taken for granted. This illustrates another layer of power and privilege difference among the participants. Which in turn reflects the power hierarchy that exists within the LGBTQIA+ community. This situation can also be viewed from MST that the Facebook structure and the culture around LGBTQIA+ activities on social media make the Hidden Identities invisible from the LGBTQIA+ activism and interaction with the LGBTQIA+ community inaccessible. Further, it can be said that, when the hidden identities are not included in the LGBTQIA+ representation in Sweden, hidden bodies are made invisible and therefore not seen in the LGBTQIA+ representation in Sweden.

In this situation, one can argue that, the hidden identities can 'remove' such friends or family who are LGBTQIA+ phobic or have threatened them (verbally or physically) from their Facebook. But, is this always that easy in every cultural situation?

In different cultures, the sense of family bonding is different. There are certain cultures, unlike the culture in Sweden, where the term family is not only used to describe the nuclear family of two parents and their children, but instead the term family extends up to relatives, and there are strong family bonds between these relatives.[56] People who are brought up in such a strong family bonding in a different social environment, for them, it becomes a hard choice to leave everything behind just because of their non-normative sexuality or gender identity. Hence, they tend to create different images of their identity that will be perceived normatively by the normative social structures around them. In case of social media, it then becomes a constant battle what they can share, or like, or which posts they can engage with. People who are in similar situation, like the

---

[56] Al-Baldawi, Riyadh, "Psykosociala konsekvenser av en förändrad familjestruktur", *Läkartidning*, 95, no. 19 (1998), 2223.

hidden identities, must self-monitor everything they do on social media. For example, if they go to a LGBTQIA+ related social gathering, then they must make sure that no one takes their photos, or if their friends are taking group photos they might need to leave it, so that it doesn't get disclosed that they have been to any LGBTQIA+ related social gathering or event. But, how many of us would enjoy self-monitoring every step of their lives, including social media (which is supposed to be a very personal free and safe space), so that their non-normative identity does not get disclosed to the wrong person?

Another point is that, some hidden identities can also be fleeing from certain oppressive structures. They stay in the fear that, if their identity gets disclosed it will put them or their families in danger. That is one reason why being visible on social media becomes an issue of safety and security for some.

However, should the situation of them not being able to be visible on social media minimize their other opportunities to be involved in the LGBTQIA+ movement and activities in Sweden? One of the participants who has hidden identity feared that people in Sweden don't have enough contextual knowledge to understand their situation.

This story is a classic example of feeling ashamed of one's own situation even though they are not responsible for this situation. This can be viewed as a MST that has been created by normative representation of the LGBTQIA+ movement in Sweden. This research did not go into investigating if there is a common expectation in Sweden that every LGBTQIA+ person in Sweden is *out and proud,* but it has identified that, the common representation of LGBTQIA+ movement on the social media does not make it clear for the hidden bodies that they are also welcome to join the community even if their identities are hidden.

One participant added another perspective:

> "It's relatives that are religious, or maybe specifically my
> aunt, otherwise our relatives are (pretty) open minded. But
> there is a certain worry all the time. I don't do that (add
> relatives on social media). I remove everything and block
> them in some cases, because there is... I sort of can't cope
> with having to debate with them. Maybe it's mostly
> (because), it is the very religious aunt (of mine), (my) biggest
> fear (is) to be rejected. I don't know if that happens, how will
> it happen, that conversation is there in my head (all the
> time)."

This segment illustrates another layer of complex intersectional experiences that hidden identities and the ones who restrict their friends and families from social media face. Not everyone who is open about themselves are open to their extended family, or in some cases even their nuclear families. Consequently, some might not post about their own identities on social media, or even they would do, they would restrict their LGBTQIA+ phobic relatives so that their identity does not get disclosed. In the interviews, it also came up that some of them are hiding their identity from their family and relatives out of love and respect towards them as they don't want to hurt their beliefs. As presented in the section 3 of this chapter, this can also be seen from Butler's theory that, to fit into normative expectation of relatives the LGBTQIA+ people sometimes may hide or perform in certain way that fits the cis-heteronormative power structure.

Hatred in Social Media

Social media is a space for everyone who has access to internet and at least a smartphone and/or computer or other device. There aren't enough sensors on LGBTQIA+ phobia and racism on social media. Even though Facebook claimed that they are working to control "hate speech"[57] on Facebook, there is no automatic (algorithmic) ban on LGBTQIA+ phobic and racist phrases. Twitter also has policies towards banning hateful speech or spreading hatred online.[58] However, neither Facebook nor Twitter can remove all the hate speech or hateful content. Therefore, these kinds of discriminatory phrases and discourses remain on social media and therefore can bring people down. However, all the participants who brought up hatred on social media have expressed that, they try to avoid such groups, posts, or people on social media. However, even if they try to avoid this, they get tagged in or added to these spaces by someone else, and once you have seen a post, you cannot un-see it.

> "I would have generally avoided the areas (social spaces) that I won't feel safe in... or I felt there is something that bugs me... There were groups in Facebook I was added to by some stupid friends for some stupid reasons... Everyday there was a thread: "is homosexuality is natural?" Then there will be bunch of cis-heteros discussing... They were not even discussing, they were blaming how you were brought up. It was mental meltdown... How stupid these people can be! Why would you even need to discuss it if it has nothing to do with you... Once... There was this guy on Twitter. (He) usually had good stuff about linguistics. Then one day he

---

[57] "Over The Last Few Weeks," Mark Zuckerberg, Facebook, last modified May 3, 2017, https://www.facebook.com/zuck/posts/10103695315624661; "Controversial, Harmful and Hateful Speech on Facebook", Marne Levine, VP of Global Public Policy, Facebook, last modified May 28, 2013, https://www.facebook.com/notes/facebook-safety/controversial-harmful-and-hateful-speech-on-facebook/574430655911054/.

[58] "The Twitter Rules," Help Center, Twitter, accessed September 6, 2017, https://support.twitter.com/articles/18311; "Hateful conduct policy," Help Center, Twitter, accessed September 6, 2017, https://support.twitter.com/articles/20175050#.

tweeted "can't people stop attacking heterosexuality?" Or whatever... I was like, we are not doing that... I ended up blocking him, because he was so annoying."

Another participant explained the frustration in being exposed to LGBTQIA+ phobic and racist comments:

> "(It) is not (that I) feel limited to do stuff, it's more like... frustration, (or) frustrating things in my life is right now... (or) people that are stupid... when I see them on social media or somewhere else I get so angry that I try to avoid them."

This participant below shared a story about how her information was spread online to publicly humiliate her:

> "In terms of when I... (got) engaged in trans feminist activism... it was firstly followed by responses coming from extremist Muslim groups... on internet... in social forums... my photographs, with my name... information about me... was public... "First Muslim transgender. First Muslim tranny. This is a shame for our Muslim community." ... Those kinds of discourses."

Dragging people into discussions such as '*is homosexuality natural*' or discussions related to religion versus LGBTQIA+ identity is another MST, "Heaping blame and putting people on shame" and "ridiculing". These experiences add to peoples' layers of suppression they are already facing in their different spaces in their life.

The question that comes from this is: who should be responsible for combating the hatreds on social media. Should it be the social media algorithm, the social media authorities, the Swedish laws or should be the responsibility of the common people to self-discipline their behaviors on social media? These questions are out of the scope of this research therefore, this research did not dig into answering these questions. This comment only gives a perspective on the complicacy around this context.

Social media: A space for separatist activism

Social media is also used as a space to be anonymous and to create closed space with other like-minded people. During the interviews, the use of social media in creating separatist group and being anonymous came up.

This participant explains how they use an Instagram account to share stories about everyday racism online, whilst they are working on creating a physical book:

> "I have (my) own organization actually. A non-profit (organization) we created last year… (there) we are about to expose everyday racism in the form of stories. So, what we want to do is that we create a book, with lots of stories from people across Sweden who talk about what they've been through. And then we would like people to be able to share in the peace and quiet, unlike online (forums)… (That) move the focus to the comment field. But a physical book can still read in peace and quiet, and you can give it away as a Christmas gift to someone who may not understand racism. And then it can read in peace and understand that "Ah, this is my neighbor and my friend" as well. I take care of our social media and I am looking for funding and looking for people who want to share their stories and stuff."

One participant expressed their tiredness in fighting the cis-heteronormative and racist structures within the LGBTQIA+ community and within Sweden. Because of this, they sought out a separatist group on social media where they could express their frustration and complex layers of experience that come with their identity.

> "I'm sort of more and more, distancing myself from white forums since it feels like there is a lack of knowledge (in those groups) ... Yeah, I no longer have the energy to cope. And (I am) following... trans-separatist forum. But I went there (because), it's more like getting into the queerhood. And I had the notion that the LGBTQ community is very aware, that it's very sort of, that it's sort of, understands cis-structure within (but) to know now in retrospect that that's not the case... But it's still white (centric)."

When asked if they have found their own separatist group this participant replied that they have created a Facebook group along with their friends to share their experiences, or to let things off their chest. Even though there is not much that take place in that group, it gives them with a way to cope up with their frustration, tiredness and the discrimination they face.

> "Me and my friend have made a Facebook group. It's not in a bigger context, but it's mine, like mine, the knowledge and experiences that I carry that I can sort of add to different communities because like, but it's also a tiredness of... Ah, well it feels like, ah like I don't have the energy, a movement that already exists and changing that from the inside where there's routines and stuff, rather create something new that's

why I have, or try to pull away from active activism. That's
where I share information nowadays."

In these closed online spaces, people have the safe environment to be themselves without having the fear to get judged and without getting attacked by their oppressors. Such functions in social media give people the tools needed to cope up with their situation, be hidden or anonymous from the outer group. As well as to organize in separatist groups to start smaller activist groups within the bigger activism sphere. It can be said that when these participants could not break the normativity and power structures around them, they made separatist spaces for themselves and other like them.

This research acknowledges the importance of such separatist closed spaces in these digital and social spaces. These small groups are the product of contextual needs in specific set up and they could benefit from support from the wider LGBTQIA+ movement in Sweden who have funding and strategic structures. In that way, these small separatist groups could sustain themselves and can eventually accommodate the wider LGBTQIA+ community with the contextual knowledge that these small groups hold.

CHAPTER 6: PROFOUND EXAMPLES

This chapter compiles examples of quotes that give an overall picture of the intersectional experiences of the non-white and/or non-Swedish LGBTQIA+ participants. These examples are here, because they go over the boundaries of the themes that were presented in the sections of Chapter 5. The quotes in this chapter are presented together with an introduction, to give the reader context to understand the quote. However, these examples are given as the participants' raw experiences, without the project team's own reflection, so that the readers have the chance to self-reflect.

Negative experiences due to stereotyping and racism when dating
This participant was exotified and racialized in several different ways, which led
to a feeling of being a product and not a human being. In this quote, they give
examples from experiences of dating. Whilst dating, they were called a terrorist
group, a character from a movie, and a sex worker.

> "When you're dating... you get racialized, (it's) really common that... (you) get exotified many times. Like, being... a hairy Middle Eastern boy, 'oh how sexy!' for that person's white fantasies. But also with non-white people too, homosexual cis-people. Both (of them) exotify me and fetishize me. I become more of a product than a human being...
>
> A lot of Islamophobia... Other things, like calling me Taliban... or Borat? The movie.... And ridiculing my parent's culture which they have no information about. They're just saying like 'teach me Arabic', I don't even speak Arabic. How am I supposed to do that? Or, like, a lot of fetishism. I was called, Harem Boy."

Are we talking enough about racism faced by the East-Asian communities in Sweden?
This participant discussed how they experience racism from their own
perspective, and they highlight: that even within groups of people that are
racialized, there are different levels of power. Their own experience (as a person
with parents from East-Asia) is that society still sees that it is acceptable to

racialize the East-Asian community and that this needs to change.

> "It feels like, yellow face, as we call it, is extremely normalized. East Asian racism is not something that many people talk about. For example, SVT broadcasting this comedy show Nile City. I don't know if you've seen? It is a comedy show where they make fun of Asians who can't talk. So, they do very much like that, yes, stereotypical things. And stuff like they were okay because no one has opposed before, so they feel that it's okay. While if they had been wearing blackface and all, everyone would have responded and everyone would have known that it is wrong. Just within East Asian racism I feel that there is not really anyone that says it is wrong as well, so I know more that we need – We need to organize and mobilize as well.
>
> I told you that I started working as a teacher... After the summer, I started in a school or a class that is a very white. The students are like 11, 12, 13 years old. So, the first thing they did when they saw me, they began to play Chinese music on their mobiles, and one had even brought a bunch of disposable chopsticks. I don't know why but they took that kind of stuff and made fun of me as a person. I felt instantly uncomfortable as well as I wanted to be there as a teacher, but also perhaps the young teacher that they can still talk *to) about games and (such). But instead it was wrong and they focus only on my look."'

Are we too silent in Sweden?

This participant explained that in their experience, Swedes are too silent and do not discuss about questions related to politics and immigration. They feared that this silence may lead to increased prejudice. In this quote, the participant gives an example about asylum issues.

> "They are very silent. I think, too silent is not good. Sometimes we need to know each other to start a discussion. Maybe silence will make things worse. For example, refugee issues or asylum issues. Because, they (Swedes) don't discuss or talk about these issues. So, the prejudice may increase."

How becoming more aware about their own rights made this participant more comfortable and empowered

This participant illustrated that becoming more aware has helped them to become more comfortable opening up and discussing things that are wrong.

> "LGBTQ world. I have been open since a few years back only. So, I do not have enough statistics to say that it is getting better or worse. But racism and stuff... I think it's gotten better. In that, (I have) become more aware. And am not afraid to open up and to talk about things that are wrong, and don't be afraid to discuss as well as things."

Newcomers and access to health

This participant problematized how the healthcare system in Sweden is not accessible and affordable for all.

> "So, like truly, that's the only thing here, health care in a nutshell. For students, there is a huge distance (between) Swedish nationals and international students, not to mention asylum seekers that even cannot enter this (the health system)."

Being a non-normative, middle-eastern, woman

This participant discussed the complexities of being a non-normative middle-eastern woman in Sweden. Furthermore, this participant expressed that the various expectations from religious people around them, as well as, their experience from living under a religious government, created pressure on them and led them to fear religion. This participant also explained how their conservative religious counterparts had social power over them but did not have power over white Swedish people.

> "They (conservative Muslims living in Sweden) ... imagine how a girl from (the) Middle East should live. This is the kind of social pressure you know it because, it is the same context you have been grown up with. Yes, they (conservative Muslims) don't answer back to them (Westerners), but they (conservative Muslims) know how to control us (ex-Muslims and/or non-normative Muslims). Because, they (conservative Muslims) don't feel strong in front of them (Westerners)... but they have that feeling that, they have power over us.
>
> (---)
>
> I am against Islamist (people) who want to control other people. I don't know Christianity that much. Of course, I know it, but it's not that I have life experience of been discriminated because of not following their tradition... I don't feel safe among religious people until I see that they really want to respect me (for who I am).
>
> (---)
>
> Specially for the ones who have been growing up here in Western countries (that I know off) ... None one of them have this experience living under (an) Islamist government for decades. And, again, I understand that, my experience is specific, I cannot extend it to other Muslim countries. Personally, I am afraid of religion. Especially when it is

institutionalized. I am always afraid that, when (any) religion is in power, they will start controlling people."

Racially motivated violence in society and the academic environment

This participant shared a series of events that happened over the course of two days. These events culminated into a very negative experience of racism and other forms of discrimination from both society and within their academic environment.

"There was a person who was high or under the influence who was being extremely racist, talked to me, got closer to me, told me about how a person killed some 12-year-old refugee… and that person then pulled out a knife at me and said that 'I'm gonna stab you here in the stomach,' and that was a really uncomfortable experience.

(---)

Then the day after… or the same night, I get to hear, you might remember that terrorist attack in Trollhättan? It was the same night that that happens, and then the day after I got into the classroom and I'm shook by this. I don't want to talk to anyone… in that group, like there are just a few people that I trusted. And then at the beginning of the year we had painted portraits of each other and they were hung in the classroom. And then I see my face… and someone had put a needle inside my eye, on the portrait."

CHAPTER 7: BI INVISIBILITY IN SWEDEN AND ACADEMIA: FROM THE PERSPECTIVE OF AN IRANIAN ACTIVIST

During the project tenure, the project team got in touch with an Iranian activist, Zeynab Peyghambarzadeh living in Sweden. She is also a board member of SFQ's local branch in Malmö. She focuses a lot in bi-inclusiveness and fighting against biphobia and racism. She completed her Master's degree in gender studies from Lund University. She will soon be moving to United Kingdom to start her PhD that focuses on bisexual asylum seekers. As this research was trying to gather data on biphobia it acknowledged that Zeynab is contextually knowledgeable person to talk about it due to her activism, research, experience and her situated knowledge from being a newcomer and a non-white person in Sweden. Therefore, we made this space below for her to share her perspective. In the following text Zeynab talks about biphobia and bi-invisibility in Swedish LGBTQIA+ community and activism from the perspective of a newcomer and activist in Sweden who has also been subjected to white normativity in Sweden. She also critiques the lack of bi-inclusivity in academia.

Making Space for Invisibles

Now, after six years of living in Sweden, I am about to move to England to write my Ph.D. dissertation about bisexual asylum seekers. It can be a good time to look back and summarize my experiences as a bisexual student and an activist of color in Sweden.

I moved from Iran to Sweden on 2011 to join a Master's program in Social Studies of Gender. Studying gender, I was privileged compared with many other international LGBTQIA students, so I did not face clear forms of LGBTQIA-phobia in university. The focus of our program was on intersectionality. We had a lot of interesting texts about queer theory and some texts about homosexuality and homophobia, but as much as I remember there was nothing about bisexuality nor biphobia.

"Can the Subaltern Speak?"

"Can the Subaltern Speak?" is a title of a famous postcolonial article from Gayatri Spivak which I find very relevant in this segment.[59] It was the first year that non-European students were supposed to pay tuition fees, so in our class there was just few non-European students and among them, all had scholarships. Although we had texts about racism, almost all the course materials were Western-centric, so I decided to take an elective course at the Center of Middle Eastern Studies. In this research and education center, many of the white lecturers and students were

---

[59] Spivak, Gayatri Chakravorty, "Can the Subaltern Speak?" in *Marxism and the Interpretation of Culture*, Cary Nelson (ed.) & Lawrence Grossberg (ed.), (Urbana and Chicago: University of Illinois, 1988), 271-314.

multiculturalist. However, it was common to talk in a way as if Middle Eastern students who were critical toward their culture are brainwashed by Western culture and cannot understand the majority Muslim inhabitants of Middle East. Therefore, I was always asking why Western social activists can question their culture but we are not allowed to critique our own culture?

Informal Student Life

I learned the word bisexual when I went from Qom, the most religious city of Iran, to the capital city, Tehran, to study. I started a Bachelor's program in Social Research on 2003 at Tehran university, which has always played a central role in the political and social movements in contemporary Iran. Living in one of the few countries that consensual same sex acts are punishable by death, of course we did not have anything about bisexuality in our formal course literature. However, the informal student life helped me to discover more about my sexuality. Meeting people from bigger cities and having more access to online spaces and rare or forbidden books helped me to find new words such as bisexuality and biphobia to explain my personal feelings and experiences.

In that sense, my student life in Tehran was similar to my student time in Sweden. I learned more about the queer perspective, non-monogamous relationships, and questioning mainstream modern romantic love by hanging out in the weekly Ronja cafe in Smålands nation in Lund. Many of students who were running the café were seniors in gender studies from different European countries. I also learned about safer sex in Project Sex (P6).

Integration

In the fourth and last semester of my Master's program, I applied for a cohabitation (sambo) visa and started to get more in contact with the Swedish society. After receiving my new residence permission, I visited the job office (Arbetsförmedlingen), I was told that I cannot get help through any program in the job office, because I have already been in Sweden for more than two years, and that I was supposed to learn Swedish and integrate in society during that time. I said to them "But I was studying in English full time and I was not sure if I can stay in this country or not," to which I got no answer.

My counselor at the job office was not good at English and I had to take my partner or friends to interpret for me. I wanted to start an internship in a cultural center but my counselor told me I can go to an internship only if I can speak Swedish with her. I asked, "But until that time, how can I integrate in society? How can I earn money?" She replied, "Ask your husband to support you". I said, "I do not have any husband". She replied, "However, your sambo should support you". I tried to change my counselor but I could not. A few months later, she finally signed my internship letter. My partner asked her, "Why you did not accept it six months ago?" To which she replied: "Because first she needed to look for a job and then if she could not find any, we could help her." "It was not obvious that someone who do not speak Swedish cannot find a job? It is not even easy for native Swedes", my partner asked. No answer.

Stuck between Cis-heteronormativity and white privilege

Going to the Swedish class was not easy. I had the same problem in taking English courses in Iran. It was quite different than studying social science at university with classmates and professors who are supposed to criticize norms or at least be aware that norms are socially constructed. In one of the biggest adult schools in Malmö, our classmates were mostly educated but from different intersectional backgrounds. On the one hand, I was still under the pressure of the traditional culture of my region. Other Middle Eastern students were still asking me questions that were built up on expectations me being perceived as a Muslim woman from the Middle East which I assume my other white friends will not get: "Why do you not marry? When do you want to have children? Why do you cut you hair short? Is it because you have cancer? Are you fasting? Are you a Shia Muslim or a Sunni one?" et cetera.

On the other hand, we all as immigrants were supposed to integrate and even assimilate in the new Western culture. Our teacher was an old feminist Swedish woman who wanted to dictate everything to us: "Open your notebook and write these words, asking a guy: "Are you writing down the words in your phone? Put your phone down and open your notebook!" "Now, close your notebooks and open your books." "Buy a package of papers with alphabet letters on them to organize your papers." As if we were young children. Maybe because she used to work at the elementary school before, or maybe because she was a white woman educating people of color how to behave. Once, when we were learning words about face appearance, the teacher said to an Afghan young woman: "I wish one day we could see your hair to see which color it is." No one said anything, maybe because it was hard for us to talk as beginner Swedish speakers. Some of us could speak English as well, but still, we all remained silent.

I did not question her for her controlling behavior but when in a private feedback meeting before summer holiday I informed her that I am changing my school together with one of my classmates because it is not easy for us to study together with the traditional religious classmates. She said, "*It can be good for you as a sociologist to know this group of people better*". I replied, "*I have lived all of my life with them and I ran away from them*". However, I did not tell her that her controlling attitude is also a part of the reason that I do not want to stay school.

A new SFI school: More open but still not good enough

My friend and I, changed our public school to a private leftist one. The students were almost the same, but at least, we had leftist teachers who were happy to help students in any aspects of their lives: to buy something online for a cheaper price or to contact social services and discuss financial issues with them. We were still supposed to learn about the Swedish royal family, but at the same time we could make fun of them. We were still learning about the health system but we were criticizing the long queues together with our teachers.

Before the Christmas holiday, I had a private feedback meeting with one of my teachers. I told her that I changed my school because of my previous classmates but that the new ones are not really different. She said, "*I realized that you are lesbian because you wrote in one of your writing assignments that you were in Pride during weekend*". I had to explain I am bi as I always have to explain it to both heterosexuals and homosexuals. Then, we talked about how students were even uncomfortable watching a Swedish movie which had some love scenes between a man and a woman, as well. Some months later, I met her in the street with her female partner. I was not studying in that school any more, and she was not working there either, so she came out to me as a lesbian, but she was trying to hide it in school by referring to her sambo with a male pronoun all the time. Soon I realized she is a LGBT activist as well, but we never had chance to talk about her experiences of being a lesbian SFI teacher.

Finding an LGBT Community

RFSL Malmö decided to start a Swedish course for newcomers, but of course it was just few hours a day, run by volunteers and could not continue after a while. At least during the recent years that I have been active in RFSL, women have not been interested to attend RFSL events in Malmö. Like many other cities, women in Malmö have their own separatist meetings, but in comparison with RFSL meetings, women-only meetings are: less regular, mostly white, information about these meetings is not available in English, and in many cases meetings are not free. Consequently, newcomer women do not have any separatist event where they can feel welcomed, yet. Until recently, the most common meeting for women that I know of was lesbian breakfast. I was told by organizers that by the word "lesbian" they mean every woman who is attracted to women, but many attendees were surprised that I am not a lesbian but a bisexual woman. They were also mostly white native Swedish speakers, who have known each other for long time. I also tried to go to non-binary queer meetings, but I did not feel welcomed there, either. It was again too Swedish and too white for me.

In August 2016, I was invited to talked about bisexuality in Malmö Pride in English. Exactly at the same time, there was another session about bisexuality in Swedish, presenting a research project done by RFSU (the Swedish Association for Sexual Education). It was exciting to have two sessions about bisexuality in two different languages, after having no session at all or just informal chatting sessions about bisexuality during the past few years in Malmö pride. However, people had to choose to go just to one of them. After the sessions, a Swedish lesbian friend of mine who was attending the Swedish lecture told me that Swedish presentation made her understand that what I was saying about biphobia in the past is important. As if she needed to hear it from a Swedish person to believe it that bisexuals have problems even in Sweden.

Lack of bi-inclusivity: In academia and activism

I asked the Malmö Pride 2016 organizers why the only sessions about bisexuality should be exactly at the same time? One of the organizers replied most sessions are about LGBT, so these two sessions are not the only ones about bisexuality. I wish, one day, general LGBT sessions would be bi-inclusive! Then, maybe we do not need to organize separate sessions to talk about biphobia. A research done on 2014 by The Public Health Agency of Sweden (Folkhälsomyndigheten) showed that the young bisexual women have the worst mental health situation among different group of homo- and bisexual people in Sweden.[60]

This confirms results of researches in other Western countries and shows that why we need to be more bi-inclusive.[61]

---

[60] Folkhälsomyndigheten, *Utvecklingen av hälsan och hälsans bestämningsfaktorer bland homo- och bisexuella personer: Resultat från nationella folkhälsoenkäten, Hälsa på lika villkor,* (Stockholm: Strömberg, 2014), 8-11.

[61] Barker, Meg, Richards, Christina, Jones, Rebecca, Bowes-Catton, Helen, Plowman, Tracey, with Yockney, Jen, and Morgan, Marcus. *The Bisexuality Report: Bisexual Inclusion in LGBT Equality and Diversity,* (Milton Keynes: The Open University, CCIG and Faculty of Health and Social Care, 2012); Conron, Kerith J., Mimiaga, Matthew J., and Landers, Stewart J., *A Health Profile of Massachusetts Adults by Sexual Orientation Identity: Results From the 2001-2006 Behavioral Risk Factor Surveillance System Surveys,* (Boston: Massachusetts Department of Public Health, 2008); Conron, Kerith J., Mimiaga, Matthew J., and Landers, Stewart J., "A Health Profile of Massachusetts Adults by Sexual Orientation Identity: Results from the 2001-2006 Behavioral Risk Factor Surveillance System Surveys", (Paper presented at the Bi Health Summit, Chicago, IL, August 13-14, 2009); Conron, Kerith J., Mimiaga, Matthew J., and Landers, Stewart J., "A Population-Based Study of Sexual Orientation Identity and Gender Differences in Adult Health." *American Journal of Public Health* 100, no. 10 (October 2010): 1953–1960; Dodge, Brian and Sandfort, Theodorus G.M., "A

Later, on September, I came back to Lund to take two interesting courses about gender equality in Scandinavia. Once, one of our lecturers was talking about same sex marriage, but as it is common, he referred to it as gay marriage. After the class, I reminded him that not everyone who marries a person of the same sex is gay. He said that when he published his book on same sex marriage in Scandinavian countries, his publisher insisted on using the phrase "gay marriage" in the title, believing it would attract more audiences. His book which is called "Odd Couples: A History of Gay Marriage in Scandinavia", was one of our course literature. Bisexuality was mentioned just few times in the book, but anyway, it was one of the rare texts among my course literatures in Sweden mentioning bisexuals as a specific group with specific needs. The book even mentions biphobia in the gay and lesbian communities.[62]

I was excited to be back in Lund, so I joined Smålands nation and P6 again. On the international bi-visibility day on September 23, I organized three events in different organizations, including RFSL Malmö, P6 and Smålands nation. In all the events, I used a short funny quiz, designed by a member of a Danish bisexual group, Bigruppen, which was used few months ago in an event at Malmö university. The first two events went very well, but the organizers of Smålands nation were not happy with the questions. As usual, I was told bisexual is a binary term and cannot be interpreted in a non-binary way. The fact that many bisexual activists and bi people interpret this word in a non-binary way, was not convincing for them. I was even told that terms like homo-flexibility are

---

Review of Mental Health Research on Bisexual Individuals When Compared to Homosexual and Heterosexual Individuals" in *Becoming Visible: Counseling Bisexuals Across the Lifespan,* ed. Beth Firestein (New York: Columbia University Press, 2007), 28-51; Shearer, Annie, et al. "Differences in Mental Health Symptoms Across Lesbian, Gay, Bisexual, and Questioning Youth in Primary Care Settings," *Journal of Adolescent Health* 59 (April 2016) 38-43, http://10.1016/j.jadohealth.2016.02.005.

[62] Rydström, Jens, *Odd couples: A History of Gay Marriage in Scandinavia,* (Amsterdam: Amsterdam University Press, 2011).

homophobic.

An International Student Again

Now that I am leaving Sweden at least for a while, I know I will miss my friends in the newcomer's community in RFSL Malmö, but I am excited to have the chance to join a bisexual community in England for the first time in my life. A community where people are not just divided to heterosexual/homosexual, and we can talk about our shared experiences of monosexism. Somewhere that I can feel normal and do not have to justify myself all the time. However, I know that there is not such a paradise in the world. We are all at the intersection of different inequality systems and no identity based group can cover all aspects of our needs. All groups need to become more accepting and diverse, and at the same time, every marginalized group needs a space of their own where they can feel safe.

CHAPTER 8: CLOSURE

This chapter presents the conclusion followed by a summary of the findings from chapter five to seven. Later in this chapter, there is a critical reflection of the results from this research, after this the limitations are presented. Finally, this chapter ends through recommendations for the way forward.

The conclusion from this research is that, it is the discourses in the power structure that create and maintain racism and discrimination against LGBTQIA+ people *within the social spaces that non-Swedish and/or non-white LGBTQIA+ people living in Sweden move within.* This is in line with how Butler[63] and Foucault[64] look at discourse and power structure. Through the application of Butler's performativity theory[65] and Ås's Master Suppression Techniques (MST)[66], this research has shown how layers of suppressions and negative experiences on top of one another are situated in the power structures in different spaces. These layers of suppressions are communicated through people's everyday life: from university, to home, and in social media, and are part of the power structures that are mentioned throughout this book. These power structures are due to: white normativity, cis-heteronormativity, language, earlier experience of LGBTQIA+

---

[63] Butler, *Gender Trouble.*

[64] Foucault, The *History of Sexuality.*

[65] Butler, "Performative Acts and Gender Constitution", 519-531; Butler, *Gender Trouble,* 79 - 149.

[66] Amnéus, Eile, Flock, Steuer Rosell & Testad, *Validation Techniques and Counter Strategies,* 5 – 11.

94

activism, social media mechanisms, CSN, citizenship/residence status, and who holds the power in what context.

SECTION 1: SUMMARY OF FINDINGS

Chapter five in this book started in Section 1 with discussing sense of belonging that critiqued white normativity in Sweden based on the theories of Butler.[67] It argued how people get perceived as a Swedish person based on their appearance and name. Moreover, Section 4 in Chapter five expanded this concept from the social media perspective by showing the body politics that people with non-white and/or non-Swedish background face. These experiences lead non-white and/or non-Swedish people to struggle to defend and to evolve within their *Swedish* identity along with their other cultural-social identities.

The second-generation Swedish participants reported that they have been getting questions that criticize their Swedish identity (e.g. *where are you from?*) since their childhood. This is an extra layer of struggle in defending their Swedish identity, and this made the participants feel alienated in a country where they were born and brought up. Whereas, people with a seemingly stereotypical Swedish appearance do not face this layer of struggle and suppression, they may face other power struggles.

Section 2 (language barrier) in chapter five showed that international students in Sweden who do not speak Swedish face another layer of struggle that a Swedish speaking person does not face. This in turn makes it harder for newcomer people that identify as LGBTQIA+ to access information online about their rights of being LGBTQIA+ in Sweden or to access information about the organizations in Sweden that protect and enhances their rights related to their gender expression,

---

[67] Butler, "Performative Acts and Gender Constitution", 519-531; Butler, *Gender Trouble*, 79- 149.

gender identity and sexuality. As presented in that section, this is another level of power hierarchy that is created by the inaccessibility in the online search system. Furthermore, the research also highlighted a power structure between people who were already involved in LGBTQIA+ activism in other countries made it easier for them to join the LGBTQIA+ community in Sweden. This illustrates the different levels of power that people who have resources to be involved in, or who are involved in the LGBTQIA+ movement and community have in comparison to those who do not have the resources or who are not involved.

Section 3 of Chapter five presented findings that were specific to student life and education environment which was referred as a space that the participants moved within. This research showed that there is a power difference for participants expressing their LGBTQIA+ identity for students that had access to CSN and not access to CSN. It also showed that SFI is an education environment that many LGBTQIA+ newcomers move within. This also showed that the overall cis-heteronormative structure in SFI, lead to the participants not receiving support in terms of LGBTQIA+ questions from the SFI environment as well as that some staff reinforced cis-heteronormativity in SFI. It resulted in the LGBTQIA+ newcomers struggling to learn Swedish, hiding their identity to fit the normative structure, or to not feeling safe in this learning environment. Furthermore, this section showed that the cis-heteronormativity, homophobic comments, racism, and white-normativity in the education environment led to participants toning themselves down and drained participants from energy to fight, complain, and continue their education.

Together, these different levels of power struggles that have been discussed thus far leads to the crucial finding of this research that the LGBTQIA+ people who are second-generation Swedish citizens and/or people with permanent residency have more privilege than the immigrants and asylum seekers who have temporary residence permit or are awaiting a visa decision. This research sees that, this power structure functions in a similar way to the power structure that gives white Swedes more structural privilege in Sweden than non-white Swedes and non-white people living in Sweden.

Beyond the results presented in Chapter five, in Chapter six this book also presented profound examples of quotes from the participants that gave an overall contextual picture of this research. Chapter seven discussed how biphobia and bi-invisibility exist in the Swedish LGBTQIA+ community as well as academia.

SECTION 2: CRITICAL REFLECTION

By applying Butler's performativity theory and MSTs, Chapter 5 to Chapter 7 furthers elaborates the power hierarchy and the layers of power struggles that non-white and/or non-Swedish LGBTQIA+ people experience in their everyday life within the spaces they move around.

Overall these chapters present how in different spaces and social situations non-white and/or non-Swedish LGBTQIA+ people living in Sweden find themselves in a lower position of power compared to white and/or Swedish cis-heteronormative people in Sweden.

The second-generation Swedish participants reported that they find it stressful to cope with white normativity, cis-heteronormativity and racism in the academic environment. These qualitative findings match with other research about people that identify as LGBTQIA+ and who are from a marginalized ethnic group: that this group faces extra layers of stress and struggles than their counterparts who are not from a marginalized ethnic group.[68] This added stress resulted in some participants giving up the fight against the discrimination they face, to change from studying a on campus programme to a distance based programme, or self-censoring themselves in order to survive their academic life or their overall experience in Sweden. This finding is similar to what the Swedish National Union of Students (SFS) showed in their own research. In their report, they showed that homosexual and bisexual students in Sweden think more often dropping out than

---

[68] Cochran, Susan D., Mays, Vickie M., Alegria, Margarita, Ortega, Alexander N., & Takeuchi, David, "Mental Health and Substance Use Disorders Among Latina/o and Asian American Lesbian, Gay, and Bisexual adults", *Journal of Consulting and Clinical Psychology* 75, (May 2007), 785–794, http://10.1037/a0023244; Balsam, Kimberly F. et al., "Measuring Multiple Minority Stress: The LGBT People of Color Microaggressions Scale", *Cultural Diversity and Ethnic Minority Psychology* 17, no. 2 (2011), 163, http://10.1037/a0023244.

heterosexual students.[69] That report also showed that student with non-Swedish ethnic background in Sweden think of dropping out more often and they don't feel as comfortable in the academic environment as much as students with a Swedish ethnic background.

The project team published an article named *"The assumption that Sweden has reached complete equality is wrong"* on The Local[70] (Sweden's news in English), and this was also shared by The Local on Facebook.[71] In this article, the project team presented that how due to people's non-white appearances they get questions such as 'Where are you from?' that implies that the non-white body in Sweden must be from another country. That article was received by people on Facebook with both good and critical reaction. However, most people who commented argued that it is perfectly okay to ask non-white people where they are from. This further showed the importance of this research and critiquing white-normativity in Sweden.

Additionally, this research is important because unlike other research in this field it has unfolded the different layers of oppression and power struggles from a feminist perspective.

Previous research has shown that cis-heteronormativity leads to homophobia-transphobia and homophobic-transphobic violence (this paper did not look at

---

[69] Sveriges Förenade Studentkårer, (SFS), *Klara dig själv: en rapport om studenters möjlighet att fullfölja studierna,* (Stockholm: SFS, 2008).

[70] McDonald, Rachel & Kabir, Opinion, "The assumption that Sweden has reached complete equality is wrong", *The Local - Sweden's News in English,* July 19, 2017, https://www.thelocal.se/20170719/opinion-the-assumption-that-sweden-has-reached-complete-equality-is-wrong.

[71] "All Of Our Non-White Participants...," The Local Sweden, published July 19. 2017, https://www.facebook.com/TheLocalSweden/posts/10157595312489619.

other forms of discrimination, for example biphobia).[72] Homophobia and transphobia are common terms used to describe the discrimination and violence faced by people who identify as homosexual or transgender. However, cis-heteronormativity affects anyone who is not heterosexual or not cis-gendered so it will not be out of the context to claim that, cis-heteronormativity leads to overall discrimination and violence faced by anybody who has an identity different to heterosexual or cisgender.

This book discussed from the very beginning how norms that are upheld in a certain power structure act as a placeholder for discrimination, struggles, and violence faced by anybody that is outside of the norm in different contextual spaces. To give some examples: getting drained of energy in the fight against racism, dropping off from courses, facing racial motivated violence, facing challenges in continuing in the cis-heteronormative structure at SFI, or having to share a classroom with a group of future professionals that do not have adequate knowledge about LGBTQIA+ questions or have LGBTQIA+ phobic attitudes. Discrimination is not experienced in isolation or as one-off events; this research has shown that different layers of discriminations builds on each other on different spaces and again they are linked with each other.

---

[72] Dreyer, Yolanda, "Hegemony and the Internalisation of Homophobia caused by Heteronormativity", *HTS Teologiese Studies/ Theological Studies* 63 (May 2007), 1-18, http://10.4102/hts.v63i1.197; Franck, Kevin C., "Rethinking Homophobia: Interrogating Heteronormativity in an Urban School," *Theory & Research in Social Education* 30, (2002), 274-286, http://dx.doi.org/10.1080/00933104.2002.10473195; Yep, Gust A., "From homophobia and heterosexism to heteronormativity: Toward the development of a model of queer interventions in the university classroom", *Journal of Lesbian Studies* 6, (August 2002) 163-176, http://dx.doi.org/10.1300/J155v06n03_14; Worthen, Meredith G. F., "Hetero-cis–normativity and the Gendering of Transphobia", *International Journal of Transgenderism* 17 (April 2016), 31-57, http://dx.doi.org/10.1080/15532739.2016.1149538; Lee, Cynthia & Kwan, Peter, "The Trans Panic Defense: Heteronormativity, and the Murder of Transgender Women", *Hastings Law Journal*, Vol. 66, no. 77, (December 2014), 77-132.

With this understanding and the results from this research, it can be said that, the cis-heteronormativity, white-normativity, and the norm of *Swedishness* that lead to LGBTQIA+ phobia and racism within the Swedish LGBTQIA+ community are created from the power hierarchy existing in different spaces in Sweden. This analysis has shown how this power hierarchy is created and maintained due to: the lack of representation of the diversity and struggles that exist in the LGBTQIA+ community in Sweden, the denial that contextualized oppression can be experienced by groups of people, and certain expectations that are reinforced in the process of perceiving people's identity and experience. Cis-heteronormativity and white-normativity still prevail in Sweden. This means that a person who is LGBTQIA+ and racialized faces not only LGBTQIA+ phobia and other forms of discrimination, struggle and violence, from the white-Swedish community, but that they also face similar oppressive structures in the non-white and/or non-Swedish communities in Sweden that are racialized. As it was discussed within chapters five, six and seven, even the LGBTQIA+ community is not aware of the power hierarchy among themselves. Therefore, as much as we need to identify the cis-heteronormativity and structural oppressions upheld by the white-Swedish community, we also need to critique the cis-heteronormativity that is present in diverse cultural, religious, or ethnic communities. People in Sweden need to critique the structure of the power imbalances, that have been presented in this book, by purposefully including all communities in this discussion.

"To be inclusive you need to include all."

SECTION 3: LIMITATION OF THE RESEARCH

It has been a challenge for the project team to conduct a full scale national project in English in Sweden whilst based in Umeå. However, the project team overcame this challenge with the help of the SFQ board and SFQ members. Also, although, not knowing Swedish and being in Umeå did not affect the research directly, it did influence the project in terms of getting in touch with other organizations. Moreover, it seemed that, having only 9 participants could be a downfall of this research. However, as presented in the methodology chapter, there was a diversity in the participants and therefore, the participants provided enough contextual data for the research presented in this book. Also, it must be remembered, that the focus group for this research contains many people that due to concerns for their safety and privacy did not contact us nor participate in the interviews.

SECTION 4: THE WAY FORWARD

SFQ hopes that as part of writing this book that we can empower others that have had similar experiences as well as help those without these experiences to become aware of them, in that way reducing discrimination and intolerance.

The people who have a non-Swedish and/or non-white background are subjected to the structural white-normativity and racism in Sweden. Denying this will not solve these problems. Rather, discussions must be made about in what way people uphold and reinforce the norms of *Swedishness* and white-normativity, and how this leads to racism, racialization and other discrimination for people that are non-Swedish and/or non-white. Moreover, it must be understood that, it's not only about *'do not go to a Nazi march'*, if a person does not feel safe, even in their privileged academic environment, then it means we are not doing enough as a community of LGBTQIA+ people in Sweden and as organizations or activists.

The academic spaces need to be LGBTQIA+ inclusive. If LGBTQIA+ issues are not presented and discussed in learning environments like universities then we continue to maintain the invisibility of LGBTQIA+ people and instead actually reinforce the oppressive structures that exists. Specially, the learning spaces focused specifically on newcomers in Sweden need to address LGBTQIA+ questions. Because, within the student community there are many LGBTQIA+ people that benefit enormously from learning more about their own rights and how norm-critique can be used to teach others about diversity. For example: this research specifically recommends that, SFI teachers and counsellors need to be competent in LGBTQIA+ issues and in norm-critique so that they can pass this information to their students and learn how to create safer spaces in their classrooms. Besides academic spaces, other organizations that work with newcomers need to be LGBTQIA+ inclusive. For example: a medical professional working with newcomers' health needs to be aware that there are LGBTQIA+

people who are new to Sweden and in many cases, do not feel safe coming out to professionals. Therefore, the professional needs to make the space safer for LGBTQIA+ newcomers.

The project team found it especially worrying that future professionals who will deal with the public, their health, and welfare are not always inclusive to LGBTQIA+ people in their academic space and occupation. Throughout working on this project, the project team have presented stories from students who experience LGBTQIA+ phobia from their classmates. The project team see that this is problematic because these students will soon be professionals. If these LGBTQIA+ phobic professionals take these attitudes and behaviors to the work force then they likely to discriminate their clients. For example: If a practicing doctor in Sweden believes that *being homosexual is unnatural* then how will they treat their patients who identify as homosexual? Therefore, the project team recommends that more research is done to understand the prevalence and pattern of LGBTQIA+ phobia in specific programs in the universities in Sweden. With this concrete data, work can be done to combat this LGBTQIA+ phobia.

LGBTQIA+ activists and anti-racist organizations should not paint a picture of Sweden with the one brush. We are here fighting the similar power structures that were built in different communities and conservative spaces against the less privileged group. We all have certain privileges and again some of us might be missing certain other privileges. Our fight should be about identifying those privileges from a contextual perspective and identify if we are either reinforcing or creating new oppressive structures for people. We should not try to put words in a victim's mouth, we should let the oppressed speak for themselves. Sometimes structural oppressions are difficult to be seen, but this book has shown this through layers of experiences, struggles and suppressions.

To end this book, the project team present some further recommendations that individuals and organizations can use to help make space for a diverse LGBTQIA+ community and reduce the racialization and other forms of discrimination against those that break the norms of white normativity and *Swedishness.*

Internal norm-critique and self-reflection

SFQ stresses the importance of internal norm-critique in its organization. Internal norm-critique means critiquing the norms that exist in a closed associated space. SFQ uses internal norm-critique to highlight and question the norms that exist and are reinforced in the organization, for example: during meetings, in the organization structure, representation in the organization, or what happens during fika breaks. Internal norm-critique can even be used by people to question the norms surrounding them in their daily life or in any group (work group, volunteer group, friends, class, etc.). Highlighting norms such as the cis-heteronormativity is the first step in norm-criticism.

Here are some points to consider in self-reflection and internal norm-critique:

- Reflect about your own openness to diversity of gender and sexuality. Reflect about whether you are reproducing cis-heteronormativity in your daily life. For example: Reflect about whether in your conversations you are upholding cis-heteronormativity by automatically assuming the other person's gender and sexuality. One way to be norm-critical about this is to use gender neutral pronouns when you do not know the other person's gender. Moreover, use the pronoun/s that the person explicitly wants you to use. Also, ask open questions, such as "do you have a partner" or "who did you move to Sweden with" rather than gendered questions such as "do you have a boyfriend?” or “do you have a girlfriend?”

- Reflect about your awareness of the diversity within the LGBTQIA+ community in Sweden. Who comes to mind when the “LGBTQIA+ community in Sweden” is mentioned? Even the members of the LGBTQIA+ community need to learn more about the diversity in gender, sexuality and other power relations. Accept, that within the LGBTQIA+ community, we are diverse.

- We recommend that, all people should be allowed to self-identify or self-label themselves, and that others should respect that we are all experts about our own selves. In our interviews, we saw examples where other people who lacked knowledge about the issues at hand had critiqued the participant’s own identity and the labels they use. With the help of internal norm-critique we all can learn from other’s perspectives about identity and labels.

- Reflect about your own position in the intersectional power relation that exists within Sweden. Consider that everybody can be privileged and oppressed in different ways, and that the amounts of privilege and oppression can also differ between people. Also, the members of the LGBTQIA+ community need to be aware of their own position and own limitations. Accept that as one person, you cannot always know how it is for another, accept that we need to make space for people with different experiences. Everybody should think about power relations and the way that we reproduce them, so that change can be made.

- Take care of yourself, self-care, those that are fighting power structures from multiple directions need to take care of ourselves. We cannot fight every day, and societies structures are not our fault, remember that.

How can we make more inclusive and safer spaces for the diverse LGBTQIA+ community in Sweden?

Many of these reflections come directly from the participants answers to interview questions, others come from the results of this research, whilst others highlight broad issues.

What can you do as a person?

- Support and show respect for friends, colleagues, classmates, and family members that live under marginalization: it helps us cope with the constant fight. Intersectionality has shown that it is harder for those who are both racialized and within the LGBTQIA+ spectrum, this makes it harder to have the energy for things like activism and fighting the oppression that is experienced from multiple angles: racism, white normativity, and discrimination against people who are LGBTQIA+.

- If you are in a position of power to be able to talk about diversity of sexuality and gender on any platform (with friends, on line, in the classroom, events etc.) then do this. This creates space for others that identify as LGBTQIA+ and if the space is safe enough, to share their own experiences. This also helps others, who do not have knowledge or personal experience to learn about the diversity that exists. For example: If you are a teacher, introducing the pronoun they, or hen in Swedish, when teaching about personal pronouns makes students who do not fit the gender norm (e.g. who are trans, and/or genderqueer) feel visible and included.

- If you can, start discussing the issues that come with intersectional identities: start to talk about racism, immigration, what is "Swedish", white normativity, religion, etc. Discuss what norms and stereotypes exists, and ask yourselves, why do these exist? What values and what image do we hold? Do we want these to exist? How can we change this? Discuss this together with your organization, work colleagues, friends, family, or classmates. Because, questioning white-normativity and discussing racism creates safer space for people who are battling with racism in their daily life.

- o For example: Reflect over why people ask the question "where are you from?" What do they really want to know? Is this relevant to the conversation or situation? If it is relevant to know what town a person grew up in, you can ask "Where did you grow up?" or to know if a person can speak other languages, ask "what languages can you speak?"

- Think critically about the question *"When does someone become Swedish?"*

- Accept that some people are out, and others are not. Do not pressure anybody or expect things of people based on your own experiences. But, always try to make safer spaces where possible, that gives confidence and makes people feel safe with their identity and expression.

What can the organizations do?

- If you are part of an organization or group: reflect over the representation within this group. Who runs your activities? Who decides what activities you have? Who attends your activities? Reflect over how you advertise your activities, which languages do you write in? What platforms? What do you write? For example:

o Some members of the LGBTQIA+ community want to participate in activities, but cannot communicate in English or Swedish when there are large groups, because they are still learning the language(s). To make space for this group we suggest having smaller events, or one-on-one meetings. This would be beneficial and attractive for this group, since it is often easier to listen to and understand each other, as well as providing a safer space to try a new language, when there are less people (and therefore less noise). We recommend therefore, that organizations organize small events that only few people can attend, so that this group can begin to join in on some events. Be explicit that these spaces have been made for people learning Swedish and/or English when advertising these events.

o LGBTQIA+ organizations need to advertise in ways that reach people who are new to Sweden. Having at least the basic information about the organization and whom to contact in as many languages as possible (English at the very least) as well as Swedish.[73]

o As an organization/employer, take the time to answer people that contact you in English. Even without Swedish proficiency, newcomers to Sweden have a lot of skills and knowledge that can be useful for your organization or workplace.

---

[73] This project appreciates that some organizations already do this, but we see that there are improvements to be made.

  ○ If possible, write more about how you provide a safe/safer space. Do not assume that people "know" they are welcome, if there is nothing written about people like yourself, then there is no way that you can know that.

  ○ Put competent LGBTQIA+ people with specific expertise who experience racism in positions of power to make them visible (actual decision-making power, not just for the purposes of representation). Seeing individuals that are like one's self means that you feel safer and more empowered to join yourself.

- Established organizations should make available spaces for separatist forums and support these with resources such as advertising and funding, so that they have a stable platform to work from.
- Student unions and groups that organize student events need to create spaces that are safe for all students, especially LGBTQIA+ students that are new in Sweden.
- We strongly recommend the Student Unions to be LGBTQIA+ inclusive. If there is a local branch of SFQ in a university they should try to make themselves more visible to the LGBTQIA+ students by either getting in touch with the student unions or by being visible during 'Welcome Fares' in the university campus.
- Organizations within the LGBTQIA+ community need to work together and help each other. If one organization is asking for help or has invited others to a meeting or discussion, then we should do what we can do aid them and participate. This helps us build the knowledge base in Sweden and will help the whole community forward faster. Together we are strong.

What can the organizations do for hidden identities?

Even if SFQ has local branches at different universities, some of our participants did not feel safe to join these. This is an issue that SFQ will be working on in the future and encourages other organizations to see over their own routines and norms. We recommend that other organizations consider the issues of safety as well.

Here are some specific points for organizing events for hidden identities:

- LGBTQIA+ organizations and groups need to state clearly on their website/social media, in communication with members/the public, and at events, whether their spaces are safe for people who are not-out and/or have a hidden identity. Moreover, if the organization welcomes people with hidden identities onto the organizing body (e.g. the board) communicate this in the same way.

- To make space for hidden identities on social media the admins of the LGBTQIA+ groups on social media need to think through what kinds of privacy settings they should have. Creating "secret groups" on Facebook is a way to increase security for members. If they are having "secret" groups, then they need advertise this on their Facebook page or website so that people can contact them privately to join the group.

Guidelines for organizing events

- State whether the event will be held in a closed or open space.

- Remind yourself, organizers, and participants at the start of an event to ask for people's permission before taking photos or video.

- If using a registration form, such as a when organizing a conference, you can ask the following questions in the registration form (asking in the registration form is safer for people rather than asking at the opening of the event, because in this case people need to "out" themselves as a hidden identity to the rest of the participants).

  o   If their name, photos, or any other identifiable information can be published by the organization.

  o   What name they like to use during the event

  o   If it is okay to share their details on social media, which details.

  o   If it is okay to take their photo / video during the event.

  o   When asking for 'emergency contact' you can add another question such as 'if the person know that you are involved in LGBTQIA+ community?' or 'does this person know what conference you are attending?'

List of LGBTQIA+ organizations in Sweden[74]

- The Swedish federation of LGBTQIA+ Students, SFQ (www.sfq.nu)
- The Swedish Federation for Lesbian, Gay, Bisexual, Transgender and Queer Rights, RFSL (www.rfsl.se)
- RFSL Youth (Focuses explicitly on the youth) (www.rfsl.se/om-oss/rfsl-ungdom/)
- Black Coffee HBTQ (Focuses on Black LGBTQIA+ people) (blackcoffeehbtq@stockholm.rfsl.se)
- RFSL Newcomers (Network for LGBTQ asylum seekers, stateless persons, and newcomers) (https://www.rfsl.se/en/organisation/asylum/asyl/)
- Transföreningen FPES (Transgender rights organization) (http://fpes.se)
- Transammans - förbundet för transpersoner och närstående (Organization for people who are transgender, their family & friends) (http://www.transammans.se/)
- Lesbisk makt (lesbian power) (http://lesbiskmakt.nu/)
- Black Queer Sweden (a feminist and black queer movement) (https://twitter.com/blackqueersswe)
- Svenskt Hbtq Initiativ - SQI Syd (Focuses on LGBTQIA+ ethnic minorities and newcomers) (https://www.facebook.com/pg/SQISyd)
- Kurdiska HBTQ-vänner (a community for Kurdish LGBTQ people in Sweden), (https://twitter.com/KurdistanHBTQ)
- IraQueer (An organization based in Sweden working on Iraq's queer movement) (https://www.iraqueer.org/)
- INIS - Intersex people of Sweden (http://www.inis-org.se/index-eng.php)

---

[74] One way to address the issue of not having information about existing LGBTQIA+ organizations working in Sweden, is to have a list. This list should be shared. For example: through student unions and SFQ local branches, at welcome fares and international welcome events. This will help students who are new to Sweden. This list includes organizations that the project team are aware of and that are currently active (as of June 2017).

MAKING SPACE!

Contact SFQ:

Website: www.sfq.nu

Email: info@sfq.nu

The book is also available as an e-book on SFQ's website